FAITH CLINIC

VOLUME XIX

SOUL TIES EDITION

The Reason Your Peace Left With
Someone Who Wasn't Your Promise.

DR. PATRICIA S. TANNER

IBG Publications, Inc.

Published by I.B.G. Publications, Inc., a Power to Wealth Company

Web address: www.ibgpublications.com

admin@ibgpublications.com / 904-419-9810

Copyright, 2026 by Patricia S. Tanner

IBG Publications, Inc., Jacksonville, FL

ISBN: 978-1-971850-07-8

Tanner, Patricia S.

Faith Clinic, Volume XIX- Soul Ties Edition: The Reason Your Peace Left With Someone Who Wasn't Your Promise

---

Printed in the United States of America.

DEDICATION

This book is dedicated to every person who has ever loved deeply and later realized that the connection they were holding onto was not healthy for their soul.

To those who stayed longer than they should have... who gave their heart, their loyalty, their prayers, and sometimes even their identity to relationships that slowly drained the life out of them. To those who tried to walk away but felt something invisible pulling them back. To those who whispered to themselves, *"Why can't I just let go?"*

You are not weak.
You are not crazy.
And you are not alone.

Soul ties can feel powerful, confusing, and painfully binding, but they are not stronger than the healing power of God.

This book is lovingly dedicated to the brave souls who are ready to reclaim their peace, rediscover their identity, and finally experience the freedom that comes when God untangles what was never meant to hold you captive.

May these pages help you break unhealthy attachments, restore your heart, and remind you that your soul belongs to God first.

With compassion and faith,

DR. PATRICIA S. TANNER
The Faith Doctor

DR. PATRICIA S. TANNER

TABLE OF CONTENTS

I Let Them Go.. So Why Did My Peace Leave Too?

When You Miss Someone Who Wasn't Good for You

Why Closure Didn't Close Anything

Still Triggered, Still Praying, Still Confused

I'm Healed… Except When I See Their Name

Soul Ties vs Covenant: Stop Calling Everything Destiny

The Spiritual Cost of Staying Too Long

Why God Didn't Bless What He Didn't Assign

You Can't Heal While Still Feeding the Tie

WELCOME TO THE FAITH CLINIC

Welcome. Not to a feel-good book. Not to a "manifest your peace back" moment. Not to a cute devotional you skim between coffee refills. Welcome to the clinic, the place where we stop spiritualizing what emotional attachment is, and we stop calling pain *purpose* just because it lasted a long time. If you're here, chances are you didn't lose your peace randomly. You didn't "wake up anxious for no reason. You didn't suddenly become weak in faith.

Your peace didn't disappear; it relocated. It got tied up with someone who was never meant to carry it. This clinic exists for people who:

- Did the breakup, but still feel bound
- Obeyed God outwardly but stayed attached inwardly
- Let go physically but stay connected emotionally
- Prayed, fasted, cried… and still feel tethered

And before we go any further, let's get one thing clear: ***This is not a condemnation clinic.***

This is a clarity clinic. You are not "crazy." You are not "behind." You are not "failing God." You are dealing with a soul tie, and soul ties don't dissolve just because time passed or distance happened. They require intention, truth, and healing, not denial, distractions, or spiritual bypassing. This clinic will be honest with you. Sometimes uncomfortably so. Because real healing doesn't happen where we protect attachments, it happens where we finally release them. No anesthesia. No spiritual clichés No pretending you're "over it" because you blocked the number. Only truth. Only healing. Only peace returned to its rightful owner: **you.**

Before treatment begins, we need your intake form. Be honest. This isn't graded. But it *is* diagnostic.

DR. PATRICIA S. TANNER

FAITH CLINIC INTAKE FORM

Soul Ties Assessment

Patient Name: _______________________________

(You. The one reading this.)

Primary Complaint (check all that apply):

☐ I think about them more than I want to.

☐ I miss them even though I know they weren't good for me.

☐ I feel anxious, heavy, or unsettled since the relationship ended.

☐ I keep replaying conversations in my head.

☐ I feel spiritually confused about why it didn't work.

☐ I feel lonely in a way that feels deeper than normal.

☐ I've tried to move on, but something keeps pulling me back emotionally.

☐ I pray about them more than I pray about myself.

☐ I'm scared to fully let go.

☐ I tell people I'm fine, but I'm not.

☐ I don't want them back, but I don't feel free either.

🏥 SYMPTOM DURATION

How long have you been experiencing emotional or spiritual discomfort related to this person?

☐ Less than 3 months

☐ 3–6 months

☐ 6–12 months

☐ Over a year

☐ Long enough that I'm tired of pretending it's normal

🧠 ATTACHMENT CHECK

Answer honestly. No spiritual flexing.

- I still check their social media:
  ☐ Often ☐ Sometimes ☐ Rarely ☐ Never
- I compare new connections to them:
  ☐ Yes ☐ No ☐ I hate that this is true
- I feel guilty imagining my future without them:
  ☐ Yes ☐ No ☐ I've never said this out loud
- Part of me believes letting go means I failed:
  ☐ Yes ☐ No ☐ I'm scared to answer

🙏 SPIRITUAL HISTORY

Select the statements that feel familiar:

☐ I believed God would "fix" the relationship.

☐ I confused chemistry with confirmation.

☐ I ignored red flags because I wanted it to work.

☐ I stayed longer than I should have.

☐ I asked God to remove them… but panicked when He did.

☐ I blamed myself for something God never approved.

☐ I kept asking for signs instead of accepting peace.

🩺 PRELIMINARY CLINICAL NOTES

(Read carefully, this is not an accusation)

- You did not lose your peace because you're weak.
- You did not stay attached because you're disobedient.
- You did not struggle because God abandoned you.
- You are here because attachment formed without alignment, and your soul is asking for restoration, not shame.

🖊 PATIENT CONSENT

Please initial each statement:

☐ _______ I am willing to be honest, even when it hurts.

☐ _______ I am open to healing that doesn't include reattachment.

☐ ______ I am ready to stop confusing familiarity with safety.
☐ ______ I give myself permission to choose peace without guilt.

Signature: _______________________________

(Signing this means you're done lying to yourself.)

Date: _______________________________

🏥 CLINIC NOTICE

Treatment will include:
- Emotional detox
- Spiritual clarity
- Boundary reinforcement
- Identity restoration
- Peace relocation (back to you)

Side effects may include:
- Temporary loneliness
- Emotional discomfort
- Increased self-awareness
- Decreased tolerance for nonsense
- Unexpected joy

Proceed to Chapter One when ready.
Healing begins now.

INTRODUCTION

How Your Peace Got Tangled Up In Someone Who Wasn't Your Promise

Let's clear something up immediately: You didn't "lose" your peace. Peace doesn't wander off like loose change in a couch cushion. Peace is stable. Grounded. Loyal. What happened is this, your peace followed an attachment it was never meant to serve. That's uncomfortable to hear, I know. Because most of us would rather believe peace was stolen than admit it was *loaned*. Accidentally. Gradually. With good intentions and poor discernment. We handed our emotional stability, spiritual focus, and inner calm to a connection that felt meaningful, but wasn't aligned.

This book exists because too many people are walking around blaming God for emotional chaos that came from **unhealed** attachment. We spiritualize it. We romanticize it. We call it "waiting," "processing," or "being sensitive." But deep down, we know the truth: Someone left your life, but they didn't leave your soul. And that's not because you're weak. It's because soul ties don't announce themselves when they form.

They don't show up holding red flags and warning labels. They show up as chemistry. Familiarity. Comfort. They show up as *"I've never felt this understood before."*

Soul ties form quietly, through emotional intimacy without boundaries, spiritual vulnerability without covering, physical closeness without covenant, and prolonged exposure to someone during a season when you were already hurting. By the time you realize what's happening, the tie is already there… and untangling it feels like losing a limb. That's why walking away didn't bring peace. That's why time didn't fix it. That's why prayer felt confusing instead of comforting. You didn't just lose a person. You lost a *pattern*. A rhythm. A regulator. And now your nervous system, emotions, and spirit are scrambling to recalibrate without something they leaned on, even if that something was unhealthy.

This is where most healing books fail you. They rush you into empowerment without allowing grief. They tell you to "choose yourself" without teaching you how. They shame attachment instead of treating it.

This book does none of that. This is not a "forget them and glow up" manifesto. This is not a "block them and boss up" pep talk. And it is not a "pray harder and stop being emotional" lecture.

This is a clinic. A place where we diagnose before we prescribe. Where we stop pretending emotional withdrawal is spiritual failure. Where we finally name the thing no one warned you about: Breaking soul ties hurt because they once helped you survive. Yes, you read that right.

Some of the people you're trying to detach from were never your promise… but they *were* your coping mechanism. Your distraction. Your emotional anchor in a stormy season. And when God removed them, or allowed the connection to end, He wasn't punishing you. He was protecting you from building a future on something temporary. That doesn't mean the pain isn't real. It means the purpose wasn't permanent.

This book will help you:

- Understand how soul ties form.
- Recognize why your peace left with them.
- Break attachments without breaking yourself.
- Heal without replacing the person.
- Reclaim peace without guilt.

But here's the warning label, because every good clinic has one: This process will require honesty. You won't be able to romanticize what hurts you. You won't be able to blame God for what was attachment. And you won't be able to rush healing just to avoid loneliness. There is no anesthesia here. Only truth. Only clarity. Only the kind of healing that lasts longer than distraction. If you're ready to stop confusing pain with purpose, attachment with love, and familiarity with safety, Welcome to the Faith Clinic. Next, we'll start where every real healing journey begins: The Intake Form.

And yes… It's going to ask questions you've been avoiding.

▣ FAITH CLINIC: SOUL TIE ID BRACELET PAGE

PATIENT WRISTBAND: DO NOT REMOVE UNTIL DISCHARGED

Name: ____

Diagnosis: Soul Tie — Emotional Attachment Without Covenant

Primary Symptom: Peace Misplacement

Allergies: Emotional Breadcrumbs, Nostalgia, Late-Night Texts

Triggers: Loneliness, Familiar Voices, "Just Checking On You" Messages

Restrictions:

☐ No Reattachment

☐ No Emotional Negotiating

☐ No Spiritualizing Red Flags

NOTICE:

This patient is healing.

Do not reintroduce old connections without medical clearance.

🚨 EMERGENCY RELAPSE WALLET CARD

(Fold. Carry. Read before texting.)

STOP. READ BEFORE YOU REACH OUT.

Ask yourself:

1. Am I lonely or missing *them*?
2. Am I seeking comfort or reopening a wound?
3. Will this interaction restore peace—or steal it again?

REMEMBER:

- Missing someone does not mean they belong in your future.
- Familiarity is not confirmation.
- Peace is more valuable than closure conversations.

IF YOU FEEL THE URGE TO REATTACH:

- Pause for 10 minutes
- Breathe deeply
- Pray one honest sentence
- Redirect your attention to something grounding

Emergency Truth:

You didn't come this far to bleed again.

📋 DOCTOR'S ORDERS

Soul Tie Recovery Protocol

Diagnosis: Emotional-Spiritual Attachment Residue
Prognosis: Full recovery with compliance

ORDERS EFFECTIVE IMMEDIATELY
1.   No contact unless necessary.
2.   No romanticizing past pain.
3.   No spiritual bargaining with God.
4.   No replacing the person with another person.

Prescribed Actions:
- Daily grounding prayer
- Journaling emotional spikes
- Intentional rest during loneliness
- Reinforcing boundaries without apology

Side Effects Expected:
Temporary sadness, clarity, emotional detox, peace returning slowly but steadily.

📇 30-DAY SOUL TIE RECOVERY PLAN

WEEK 1: DETOX
- Remove reminders.
- Limit emotional stimulation.
- Name the attachment honestly.
- Sit with silence without filling it.

Focus: Awareness, not relief

WEEK 2: RE-ROOTING
- Redirect comfort toward God and self-care.
- Establish new routines.
- Journal identity outside the connection.

Focus: Stability without substitution.

WEEK 3: STRENGTHENING
- Practice saying no internally.
- Reinforce boundaries emotionally.
- Notice peace returning in moments.

Focus: Self-regulation

WEEK 4: RESTORATION
- Celebrate progress
- Reflect on lessons learned
- Release guilt fully

Focus: Peace ownership

DISCHARGE DECLARATION
I reclaim my peace without guilt.
I release attachments that cost me alignment.
I trust God with my connections and my healing.

PART I:
THE SYMPTOMS

PERSONAL NOTES

Chapter 1

"I Let Them Go... So Why Did My Peace Leave Too?"

SYMPTOM

Persistent emotional unrest after separation, marked by confusion, longing, anxiety, and spiritual disorientation.

You finally did it. You let them go. You ended the relationship, created distance, or obeyed the inner nudge that told you it was time to walk away. On paper, it looks like progress. On the outside, it looks like obedience. Friends congratulate you for choosing yourself, and spiritually speaking, you may even believe you did the "right thing." Yet, instead of peace rushing in like a reward for your courage, something else arrived. Quiet. Heavy. Unsettling. An emotional static that hums beneath your daily life and refuses to turn off.

This is the symptom no one talks about because it doesn't fit the narrative of instant healing. This is the part of the story where you obeyed, but you did not immediately feel better. In fact, in some ways, you may feel worse. You wake up with a tightness in your chest that has no obvious explanation. You reply to moments in your head that you thought you had already made peace with. You find yourself missing someone you logically know was not aligned with your future, yet emotionally still feels significant. You ask God why obedience feels like loss instead of relief.

This symptom is deeply confusing because it contradicts what you expected healing to feel like. You assumed that letting go would bring immediate clarity, emotional lightness, and spiritual relief. Instead, you feel disoriented, restless, and unsettled. You may even question whether you made the right decision, not because the relationship was healthy, but because the discomfort of detachment feels unbearable at times. Your mind begins to whisper lies disguised as questions: "What if I misheard God?" "What if this pain means I walked away too soon?" "What if peace left because I chose wrong?"

What you are experiencing is not a failure of faith. It is the physiological, emotional, and spiritual response to detachment from an attachment that once regulated you. When a soul tie forms, it does not simply affect your emotions; it subtly restructures how your inner world functions. Over time, your nervous system, emotional stability, and even your sense of spiritual grounding may have become oriented around the presence, attention, or validation of that person. Their voices calmed you. Their presence anchored you. Their approval reassured you. Even their inconsistency kept you emotionally engaged.

When that connection ends, your system does not immediately recognize that the separation was healthy. It only recognizes that something it depended on is suddenly gone. This is why peace did not automatically return when the relationship ended. Peace, in this context, was not missing. It was displaced. It had been quietly outsourced to a connection that was never meant to carry it.

This symptom often manifests as emotional withdrawal. Like detoxing from a substance, your soul experiences cravings for familiarity, even if that familiarity was harmful. You may feel tempted to reach out, check their social media, replay old conversations, or imagine scenarios where things worked out differently. None of these impulses mean you are weak. They mean your soul is recalibrating after losing something it leaned on for stability.

Spiritually, this symptom can feel even more confusing. You may pray and feel disconnected. Worship may feel muted. Scripture may feel harder to engage. You may interpret this as spiritual dryness, when it is emotional grief expressing itself in spiritual language. Your spirit is not distant from God; it is exhausted from carrying unresolved attachment.

This is why peace feels absent even though you did the "right thing." Peace does not automatically return when a person leaves. Peace returns when alignment is restored. Until then, your soul is learning how to function without an emotional regulator it once relied on.

This symptom is not punishment. It is not evidence that you failed God. It is evidence that you formed a bond that mattered deeply to your inner world, regardless of whether it was meant to last. Healing begins when you stop judging yourself for feeling this way and start understanding what happened inside you.

TEACHING
Peace is not the reward for separation; peace is the result of realignment

Most people believe peace comes from removing the wrong person. While separation is often necessary, it is not the same thing as healing. Separation removes access. Healing removes attachment. Until attachment is addressed, peace remains unstable, regardless of how much distance exists.

Peace is not simply the absence of chaos. Peace is the presence of alignment. It exists where identity, boundaries, purpose, and spiritual authority are functioning in harmony. When peace left after the relationship ended, it was not because you lost something essential. It was because something essential had been misplaced long before the separation occurred.

Soul ties often form gradually and quietly. They do not require  intention or awareness. They form through repeated emotional intimacy, shared vulnerability, prolonged exposure during difficult seasons, or physical closeness without covenant. Over time, the relationship becomes more than companionship. It becomes a source of emotional regulation. Your sense of calm, reassurance, and even worth begins to fluctuate based on the health of the connection.

This is why God does not always immediately restore peace after a relationship ends. God is not interested in returning you to emotional dependence under a different name. He is interested in restoring authority. Authority over your emotions. Authority over your attachments. Authority over your peace.

Peace feels uncomfortable when authority is being returned to you because responsibility replaces reliance. When you no longer have someone to emotionally lean on, you must learn how to self-regulate, spiritually anchor, and emotionally stabilize without outsourcing that work to another person. This process is uncomfortable, but it is deeply necessary.

Many people mistake this discomfort for loneliness. It is retraining. Your soul is learning how to find stability without external reinforcement. This is why rushing to replace the person often delays healing. Replacement may soothe the discomfort temporarily, but it does not restore alignment. It simply transfers the attachment.

Healing requires you to sit in discomfort long enough to understand what the attachment provided. Was it validation? Safety? Distraction? A sense of being chosen? Once you identify what the connection is supplied, you can begin to meet those needs in healthy, grounded ways that do not compromise your peace.

God did not remove that person to leave you empty. He removed them to prevent you from building a future on something temporary. Some connections are meant to support you in a season, not sustain you for a lifetime. Letting go of them does not mean the season was meaningless. It means it was finite.

Peace returns gradually as you re-root yourself. It returns as you stop romanticizing what hurt you. It returns as you release guilt for missing someone who mattered. It returns as you stop confusing grief with disobedience. It returns as if you accept that healing does not feel empowering at first; it feels destabilizing before it feels free.

You are not broken because peace feels distant right now. You are healing. And healing does not announce itself with comfort. It announces itself with clarity.

Peace is not something you chase. It is something you reclaim by restoring alignment. And alignment begins when you stop asking why peace is left and start asking where it belongs.

💊 Faith Prescription

Reclaiming Peace Without Reattaching

This week's prescription is not about feeling better. It is about becoming honest. The goal is not emotional relief; the goal is emotional clarity. Your assignment is to stop interpreting discomfort as failure and start recognizing it as recalibration. Peace does not return through panic decisions or emotional bargaining. It returns through patience and alignment.

You are prescribed intentional pause. This means resisting the urge to reach for familiar comfort when your emotions spike. When anxiety rises, you do not reach outward; you look inward. You acknowledge the discomfort without trying to eliminate it immediately. You remind yourself that withdrawal does not mean something is wrong; it means something is being untangled.

You are also prescribed self-observation without judgment. Pay attention to when the discomfort shows up. Notice what triggers the urge to miss them. Do not shame yourself for these moments.

Simply note them. Healing accelerates when awareness replaces avoidance.

Dosage:
Daily reflection without reattachment. No emotional substitutions. No contact driven by loneliness.

🧬 Spiritual Vitamin

Identity Before Attachment

Your spiritual vitamin for this chapter is identity reinforcement. Attachments weaken when identity strengthens. Each day, you are to remind yourself, out loud if possible, that your peace is not sourced from another person. You are not incomplete because someone left. You are becoming whole because the dependency is being addressed. Repeat this truth daily: *"My peace comes from alignment, not access."*

This vitamin works slowly but deeply. Take it consistently. Skipping doses will not cause failure, but consistency will accelerate clarity.

🕊 Holy Spirit Consult

Learning to Sit with Silence

Invite the Holy Spirit into the quiet moments you usually try to escape. Ask Him not to remove the discomfort, but to explain it. Pray for understanding, not relief. When emotions rise, ask, "What are You teaching me about myself right now?" instead of "How do I make this stop?" The Holy Spirit does not rush healing. He stabilizes it. Trust that His silence is not absence, it is space being created for restoration.

🙏 Guided Prayer

(Read slowly. Do not rush this.)
"God, I admit that letting go has been harder than I expected. I thought obedience would feel lighter, but instead it feels quiet and heavy. I bring You this discomfort without trying to fix it. I ask You to show me where my peace was misplaced and help me return it to You and to myself. Teach me how to sit with this season without reattaching to what You have already released. I trust that You are not punishing me but restoring me. I receive Your peace, not borrowed, not conditional, but whole. Amen."

📝 Journal Reflection Page

Be honest. This is for healing, not performance.
Answer in full sentences. Do not edit for spirituality.

1. What part of my peace did I rely on this person to provide?

____

____

____

____

____

2. When did I first notice my peace becoming tied to their presence or attention?

____

____

____

3.   What am I most afraid of feeling if I fully let go?

____

____

____

____

4.   What would it look like to reclaim my peace without replacing the person?

____

____

____

____

____

____

____

____

____

____

Write until clarity comes, not until comfort does.

℞ Clinical Note

Progress is not measured by how little you miss them.
Progress is measured by how much less you abandon yourself.
☑ NEXT APPOINTMENT

PERSONAL NOTES

Chapter 2

"When You Miss Someone Who Wasn't Good For You"

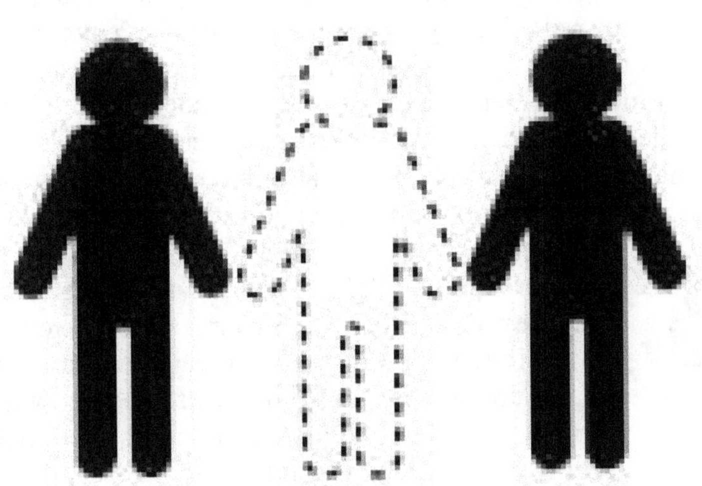

SYMPTOM
Persistent longing for a person who caused harm, confusion, instability, or misalignment, often accompanied by guilt, shame, and self-doubt.

One of the most confusing emotional experiences in healing is missing someone you know, without debate, without revision, was not good for you. This is not the romantic ache of lost love. This is not grief over something healthy that simply ended. This is the disorienting pain of longing for a connection that caused damage, instability, or spiritual compromise, yet still feels emotionally magnetic.

This symptom shows up quietly but persistently. You find yourself remembering their laugh, their voice, the way they once made you feel seen. You forget the anxiety, the emotional whiplash, the inconsistency, the red flags you explained away. Your mind selectively edits the past, highlighting moments of closeness while minimizing moments of harm. You begin to wonder whether you exaggerated the pain, whether you were too sensitive, whether maybe, just maybe, it wasn't as bad as you remember. This is where shame creeps in. You feel embarrassed that you still miss them. You  judge yourself for thinking about them. You wonder why you haven't "moved on" faster. You may even spiritualize your shame, telling yourself that missing them means you are not healed enough, faithful enough, or strong enough. You may pray for the feelings to go away, only to feel worse when they don't.

What makes this symptom especially dangerous is how convincing it feels. Missing someone can masquerade as evidence of love, destiny, or unfinished business. Your emotions argue that longing must mean something was real, significant, or meant to last. But emotions are not historians. They are storytellers, and not always truthful ones.

This symptom often intensifies during moments of loneliness and stress, or transition. When life feels quiet, uncertain, or overwhelming, your soul reaches backward for familiarity. It does not reach for what was healthy; it reaches for what was **known**. Familiarity feels safer than uncertainty, even when familiarity is harmful.

You may find yourself tempted to reach out "just to check in," replaying conversations in your head, or imagining how things could have been different if circumstances had changed. You may even feel guilt for imagining a future without them, as if moving forward is a betrayal of what you shared. What you are experiencing is not love resurfacing. It is attachment memory. Your nervous system remembers how this person once regulated your emotions. It reminds you of the relief you felt when they responded, the comfort of not feeling alone, the validation of being chosen, however inconsistent. When that regulation is gone, your system protests. It confuses relief with rightness and absence with loss.

This is why missing someone who hurt you feels so intense. Your body remembers dopamine, the emotional heights, the moments of connection that temporarily soothed deeper wounds. And now, without that stimulus, your system grieves, not because the person was good for you, but because the coping mechanism is gone.

This symptom does not mean you want them back. It means your soul is detoxing from a bond that once served a purpose, even if that purpose was survival rather than love.

TEACHING

Longing does not mean alignment. It means attachment has not finished unraveling.

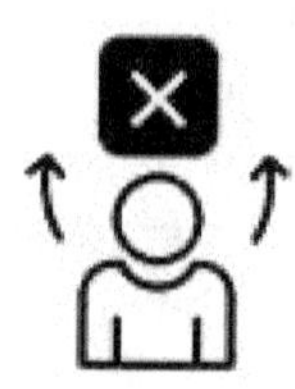

One of the most dangerous lies in emotional healing is the belief that missing someone validates the relationship. It does not. Longing is not proof of purpose; it is evidence of imprinting. When emotional bonds form during vulnerable seasons, they leave an imprint on your nervous system. That imprint does not disappear just because logic says the relationship was unhealthy.

Missing someone who wasn't good for you does not mean you misheard God. It means your soul is disentangling from a pattern it once depended on. Trauma bonding often plays a significant role here. Trauma bonds form when emotional intensity replaces emotional safety. High highs and low lows create a chemical and emotional cycle that feels powerful, even addictive. The inconsistency itself becomes the hook. Your system learns to crave resolution, validation, and relief, even when those things arrive unpredictably.

This is why healthy relationships can feel "boring" after unhealthy ones, and unhealthy ones can feel "irreplaceable" after they end. Your system is not craving the person; it is craving the stimulation.

God does not interpret your longing as disobedience. He understands that healing unfolds in layers. What He does challenge is what you do *with* the longing. Longing becomes dangerous when it is treated as instruction rather than information. Missing someone is information. Acting on it without discernment is how people relapse into cycles that cost them peace.

Healing requires you to grieve honestly without rewriting history. It requires you to hold the truth and the longing at the same time: *I miss them, and they were not good for me.* Both can be true without canceling each other out.

Peace is restored when longing loses authority. When you stop letting emotion make decisions, clarity has room to return. Over time, as your nervous system stabilizes and your identity strengthens, the longing will soften, not because you forced it away, but because your system no longer needs it.

You are not wrong for missing them. You are wrong only if you let missing them convince you to abandon yourself again. Healing does not erase memory. It rewrites meaning.

Faith Prescription

Allow Longing Without Obedience To It

This week's prescription is restraint with compassion. You are not required to eliminate longing; you are required to stop obeying it. When the feeling arises, acknowledge it without acting on it. Say to yourself, "I miss them, and I still choose peace." You are prescribed emotional pause. No reaching out. No nostalgic spirals. No romantic rewriting. Let the feeling rise and fall without intervention. This is how detox works.

Dosage: As needed when longing appears. No emotional bargaining. No self-shaming.

Spiritual Vitamin

Discernment Over Desire

Your spiritual vitamin for this chapter is discernment. Desire speaks loudly. Discernment speaks clearly. Each day, remind yourself that feelings are real but not authoritative.

Repeat daily: *"I honor my feelings without letting them lead me."*

🕊 Holy Spirit Consult

Separating Memory From Meaning

Ask the Holy Spirit to help you remember accurately, not selectively. Invite Him to bring truth to memory without shame. Ask Him to remove the emotional charge from moments that no longer serve your future.

🙏 Guided Prayer

"God, I bring You my longing without trying to justify it. I acknowledge that I miss someone who was not aligned with my peace. Help me hold this feeling without letting it pull me backward. Heal the places in me that are attached for survival instead of safety. Teach me how to grieve without returning. I trust You to restore clarity where confusion once lived. Amen."

📝 Journal Reflection Page

1. What do I miss most? The person, or how they made me feel?

____

____

____

____

____

2. What needs did this connection temporarily meet?

____

____

____

____

____

____

3. What truth about the relationship do I tend to minimize when I feel lonely?

____

____

____

____

____

4. How can I honor my healing without acting on nostalgia?

____

____

____

____

5. Write until the emotion loses power.

____

____

____

____

⚕ Clinical Note

Missing someone does not mean you belong with them. It means your system is healing from dependency.

☑ **NEXT APPOINTMENT**

PERSONAL NOTES

Chapter 3

"Why Closure Didn't Close Anything"

SYMPTOM

Persistent emotional unrest after conversations meant to bring peace, clarity, or finality, often marked by renewed confusion, emotional regression, and reopening of wounds.

You had the conversation. You said what needed to be said. You finally "cleared the air." And yet, instead of relief, you felt heavier. This symptom is one of the most frustrating experiences in emotional healing because it directly contradicts what you were promised. You were told that closure would bring peace. You were told that one honest conversation would help you move on. You were told that clarity comes from explanation, mutual understanding, or one last exchange of truth. So, you gathered courage, prepared your words, and reentered a connection you were trying to leave, believing it would finally set you free. Instead, everything reopened. You walked away from the conversation replaying sentences in your head, questioning your tone, wondering if you said too much or not enough. You felt emotionally exposed rather than resolved. You may have even felt pulled back into emotional intimacy you were trying to escape. The conversation did not close the chapter; it expanded it.

This symptom shows up as renewed attachment after contact. You feel mentally preoccupied again. You analyze their responses. You assign meaning to their silence or their words. You wonder whether

the conversation meant more to them than they admitted. You feel tempted to continue the dialogue because it feels unfinished, even though you have already tried to finish it. What makes this symptom so disorienting is that it feels reasonable. Seeking closure sounds mature. Wanting clarity sounds healthy. Expressing feelings sound honest. But what you experienced was not healing; it was ***re-engagement***.

Closure conversations often reopen wounds because they are rarely about information. They are about validation. They are hoping the other person will finally acknowledge your pain, your value, or their role in the damage. When that acknowledgment does not come, or comes inconsistently, it deepens the wound rather than sealing it.

This symptom is intensified when the relationship already involves emotional imbalance, avoidance, or inconsistency. In those dynamics, closure becomes a moving target. You keep returning for answers that were never going to be given clearly because the relationship itself was unclear. 

Spiritually, this symptom can feel like a setback. You may tell yourself that you have made progress. You may feel ashamed for reopening communication. You may even blame yourself for "knowing better" and still reaching out. But shame does not heal this symptom. Understanding does. What you encountered was not a lack of closure. It was the reality that closure is not something another person can give you.

TEACHING
Closure is not an agreement. It is a decision.

One of the most common misconceptions in emotional healing is the belief that closure requires cooperation. It does not. Closure does not require the other person to understand you, validate you, or admit wrongdoing. Closure requires authority to stop seeking resolution from someone who could not offer stability in the relationship itself.

When relationships end without clarity, the mind tries to manufacture resolution through conversation. But conversations cannot fix what was never grounded. If communication was inconsistent during the relationship, it would not become healthy at the end. If accountability was absent before, it will not suddenly appear when the relationship dissolves. This is why closure conversations often reignite emotional attachment. They recreate intimacy. They reopen vulnerability. They place your healing back in someone else's hands. Instead of sealing the wound, they disturb it.

God does not ask you to understand everything before you move forward. He asks you to trust Him when understanding is incomplete. Some endings are intentionally unclear, not to torment you, but to teach you how to walk away without consensus.

Healing happens when you stop negotiating your peace. Closure becomes possible when you accept that the absence of explanation is itself information. The lack of accountability is clarity. The inability to meet you emotionally is the answer you were seeking.

Peace does not come from the last conversation .Peace comes from the last decision. When you stop returning for explanations, your nervous system slowly recalibrates. When you stop reopening emotional doors, your soul begins to stabilize. Closure happens internally, not interpersonally. You do not need one more conversation. You need permission to stop explaining yourself. And that permission comes from truth, not agreement.

🔖 Faith Prescription

Ending Conversations That Reopen Wounds

This week's prescription is emotional finality without dialogue. You are prescribed silence, not as avoidance, but as protection. You are to stop seeking peace through explanation. When the urge to clarify arises, remind yourself that clarity does not come from repeating the past.

Dosage: No follow-up conversations. No "one last message." No emotional footnotes.

🧬 Spiritual Vitamin

Authority Over Understanding

Your spiritual vitamin for this chapter is authority. Understanding feels comforting, but authority is stabilizing. Each day, I affirm that you do not need answers to move forward.

Repeat daily: *"I choose peace even without explanation."*

🕊 Holy Spirit Consult

Releasing The Need To Be Understood

Ask the Holy Spirit to help you release the need to be fully understood by someone who could not fully show up. Invite Him to soothe the part of you that equates explanation with worth.

🙏 Guided Prayer

"God, I release the need for closure that depends on another person. I surrender my desire to be understood, validated, or agreed with. Help me trust that silence can be holy and final. Heal the places in me that keep returning for answers instead of rest. I choose peace over explanation. Amen."

📝 Journal Reflection Page

1.   What am I still hoping they will say or admit?

____

____

____

____

____

____

2. How has seeking closure reopened emotional wounds?

____

____

____

____

____

____

____

____

____

3. What would it look like to give myself closure?

____

____

____

____

____

4. What truth am I avoiding by wanting one more conversation?

____

____

____

____

____

____

____

____

____

____

____

____

____

Write until authority replaces longing.

⚕ Clinical Note

Closure is not something you receive. It is something you decide.

☑ **NEXT APPOINTMENT**

PERSONAL NOTES

Chapter 4

"Still Triggered, Still Praying, Still Confused"

SYMPTOM

Emotional and spiritual disorientation marked by recurring triggers, unanswered prayers, and the feeling that faith is not working the way it used to.

One of the most discouraging symptoms in the healing process is the moment you realize that prayer has not eliminated your emotional reactions. You are still getting triggered. You are still reacting internally to memories, places, phrases, and people connected to what you are trying to heal from. You are still having emotional spikes that feel disproportionate to what is happening in the present moment. And what confuses you most is that you are praying through it. You are not avoiding God. You are not rebelling. You are not ignoring your spiritual life. In fact, you may be praying more than ever. You are asking God for peace, clarity, emotional stability, and direction. Yet triggers continue to surface. Certain songs, dates, locations, or even random thoughts can suddenly pull you back into emotional turbulence. Your body reacts before your logic does. Your heart races. Your chest tightens. Your mood shifts. And you find yourself wondering why prayer hasn't "fixed" this yet.

This symptom creates deep spiritual confusion because it makes you question your faith rather than your healing stage.  You may begin to wonder whether you are praying incorrectly, believing incorrectly, or missing something spiritually essential. You may silently ask yourself why God seems quiet while your emotions are loud. You may even feel frustrated with yourself for still reacting to things you thought you were over.

What you are experiencing is not spiritual failure. It is emotional memory surfacing during a season of recalibration. Triggers are not evidence that healing has failed. They are evidence that healing is in progress. A trigger is simply a reminder that your nervous system learned something in a previous season that it has not yet unlearned. Prayer does not instantly erase that learning. Prayers support the process of retraining it.

This symptom feels especially disorienting because prayer is often misunderstood as a bypass instead of a partnership. You may have unconsciously expected prayer to remove the discomfort rather than guide you through it. When that does not happen, frustration sets in. Confusion follows. And doubt begins whispering that something must be wrong with you or your faith. But nothing is wrong with you.

Your spirit may be willing, but your nervous system is still catching up. Emotional healing does not happen at the same pace as spiritual conviction. Triggers linger not because God is absent, but because your body and emotions are still learning safety outside of old patterns.

TEACHING
Prayer does not erase triggers; it re-educates the soul.

One of the most important truths you must understand in this season is that prayer is not anesthesia. God does not numb you through prayer. He transforms you through awareness, patience, and process. If prayer instantly erased every emotional response, healing would never reach the deeper layers of your soul where patterns are formed. Triggers exist because your system learned how to survive in a particular environment.

Those reactions were once protective. They helped you navigate uncertainty, emotional instability, or relational inconsistency. Now that the environment has changed, your system needs time to learn that it no longer must respond the same way. God is not confused by your triggers. He is not offended by your questions. He is not disappointed that you still feel what you feel. He understands that healing unfolds in stages. Spiritual clarity often comes before emotional stability, not after.

Prayer works by bringing alignment, not immediate relief. When you pray during triggering moments, you are not asking God to remove the reaction. You are inviting Him to teach your soul a new response. Over time, that response becomes instinctual. Peace replaces panic. Awareness replaces reactivity.

This is why prayer sometimes feels ineffective during healing  seasons. It is not that nothing is happening. It is that something slow and foundational is happening. Your soul is being retrained to feel safe without familiar chaos. That kind of transformation takes repetition, not performance.

Healing deepens when you stop asking why you are still triggered and start asking what the trigger is revealing. Triggers are teachers. They show you where attachment still lives, where fear still speaks, and where identity is still being restored. Prayers do not fail because triggers exist. Prayer works *with* triggers to build something stronger than emotional reactivity, spiritual stability. Peace grows where understanding replaces judgment.

💊 Faith Prescription

Responding Instead of Reacting

This week's prescription is conscious response. When a trigger surfaces, you are not to shame yourself or suppress the feeling. You are to pause, breathe, and name what is happening. You are prescribed awareness over avoidance. Do not rush to fix the emotion. Let it inform you. Healing accelerates when reaction slows.

Dosage: As needed during emotional spikes. Pause before responding. Name the trigger without judgment.

🧬 Spiritual Vitamin

Patience With The Process

Your spiritual vitamin for this chapter is patience. Healing does not move at the speed of desire. It moves at the speed of safety. Each day, remind yourself that progress is happening even when it feels slow.

Repeat daily: *"God is not late in my healing."*

🕊 Holy Spirit Consult

Understanding Without Condemnation

Ask the Holy Spirit to help you interpret your triggers without condemnation. Invite Him to show you what is being healed instead of focusing on what feels broken.

🙏 Guided Prayer

"God, I bring You my confusion and my triggers. I release the belief that prayer should erase my feelings instantly. Teach me how to respond with awareness instead of fear. Help me trust that You are working even when the process feels slow. I receive Your peace as a teacher, not an escape. Amen."

📝 Journal Reflection Page

1. What situations or memories trigger me most often?

____

____

____

____

____

2.   What do these triggers reveal about what I am still healing?

____

____

____

____

____

3.   How have I judged myself for still reacting emotionally?

____

____

____

____

____

____

4.   What would it look like to respond with patience instead of panic? Write until clarity replaces frustration.

____

____

____

____

____

⚕ Clinical Note

Triggers are not setbacks. They are invitations to deeper healing.

☑ **NEXT APPOINTMENT**

PERSONAL NOTES

Chapter 5

"I'm Healed… Except When I See Their Name"

SYMPTOM
Sudden emotional spikes triggered by reminders of a past connection, often interpreted as relapse, failure, or proof that healing was never real.

One of the most demoralizing moments in the healing process happens when you genuinely believe you are doing well, until something small shatters that confidence. You can go for days or even weeks feeling grounded, emotionally stable, and spiritually clear. You may even begin to trust that healing is finally working. Then, without warning, their name appears on your phone, in a conversation, or on a screen, and your body reacts before your mind can intervene. Your stomach tightens. Your chest feels heavy. Your thoughts are scattered. And immediately, shame follows. You tell yourself that if you were truly healed, this wouldn't affect you anymore. You question your progress. You wonder whether all the emotional work you have been doing was an illusion. You may even spiral into self-criticism, accusing yourself of backsliding or being emotionally weak.

This symptom is particularly painful because it feels like betrayal, by your own body. You did not invite the memory. You did not choose the reaction. It happened automatically. And because it happened automatically, it feels like proof that the attachment is still stronger than you're healing. But this reaction is not evidence of failure.

It is evidence of residual imprinting. Your nervous system stores emotional memory differently than your conscious mind. Healing begins cognitively and spiritually before it completes itself neurologically. This means you can understand the truth, make healthy decisions, and still experience involuntary emotional responses when something reminds your system of a former attachment.

Seeing their name activates memory, not desire. It activates association, not intention. Your body remembers a pattern before your mind has time to contextualize it. That momentary reaction does not mean you want them back. It means your system has not fully unlearned the association yet.

What makes this symptom so destabilizing is the meaning you attach to the reaction. Instead of acknowledging it as a natural part of healing, you interpret it as regression. You begin to monitor yourself obsessively, watching for reactions as if they ae diagnostic tests. This hypervigilance keeps your nervous system on edge and slows healing rather than supporting it.

This symptom often leads people to emotional avoidance. You may start trying to control your environment excessively, avoiding places, conversations, or people that might remind you of them. While some boundaries are healthy, excessive avoidance reinforces fear rather than resilience. Healing does not require the elimination of all reminders. It requires retraining your response to them.

TEACHING
Healing is not the absence of reaction; it is the restoration of regulation.

One of the most damaging myths in emotional recovery is the belief that healing should be linear and symptom-free. Healing is cyclical. It unfolds in layers. Progress shows up as shorter reactions, faster recovery, and increased self-awareness, not emotional numbness.

Seeing someone's name and feeling a reaction does not mean the soul tie is intact. It means the imprint is still dissolving. Imprints fade through repetition of safety, not through force or judgment.

God does not measure your healing by how little you react. He measures it by how quickly you return to peace. The difference between being bound and being healed is not whether you feel something, it is whether that feeling controls you.

When you respond to a trigger with panic or shame, you reinforce  the association. When you respond with calm acknowledgment, you weaken it. This is how the nervous system learns that the stimulus no longer requires alarm. Healing accelerates when you stop monitoring yourself for perfection and start allowing your system to recalibrate naturally. Emotional regulation is learned through exposure and safety, not avoidance and fear.

Spiritually, this chapter is about understanding grace in the healing process. God does not expect instant mastery over emotional memory. He expects willingness, honesty, and patience. He does not withdraw peace because your body reacts. He invites peace to teach your body a new language.

Each time you see their name and choose not to spiral, not to reach out, not to shame yourself, you are practicing freedom. Each non-reaction is a small victory, even if your emotions initially rise. Healing does not erase memory. It removes authority. And authority is reclaimed one regulated moment at a time.

💊 Faith Prescription

Regulation Over Reaction

This week's prescription is nervous system regulation. When a reminder appears, you are to pause and ground yourself instead of interpreting the reaction. Breathe slowly. Remember that a reaction is not a command.

You are prescribed self-compassion during emotional spikes. Shame delays healing. Kindness accelerates it.

Dosage: As needed when triggered. Pause, breathe, and re-center. No self-judgment.

🧬 Spiritual Vitamin

Grace for the Process

Your spiritual vitamin for this chapter is grace. Healing is not measured by perfection. It is measured by persistence.

Repeat daily: *"A reaction does not undo my healing."*

🕊 Holy Spirit Consult

Teaching Body Safety

Invite the Holy Spirit to partner with you in moments of emotional activation. Ask Him to help your body feel safe in the present moment, not threatened by memory.

🙏 Guided Prayer

"God, I release the belief that healing means never reacting. Help me respond calmly instead of shame when memories surface. Teach my body that it is safe now. I trust You to complete what You began in me. I receive grace for this process. Amen."

📝 Journal Reflection Page

1. What reminders trigger emotional reactions for me?

____

____

____

____

____

____

2.   How do I usually interpret these reactions?

____

____

____

____

____

3.   What would change if I stopped judging myself for feeling them?

____

____

____

____

____

4.   How can I practice calm regulation instead of panic? Writing until reassurance replaces fear.

____

____

____

⚕ Clinical Note

Healing is not proven by silence. It is proven by stability.

☑ NEXT APPOINTMENT

PERSONAL NOTES

PART II:
THE DIAGNOSIS

PERSONAL NOTES

Chapter 6

"Soul Ties vs. Covenant: Stop Calling Everything Destiny"

SYMPTOM

Chronic confusion between emotional intensity and divine alignment, often expressed through spiritual language that justifies unhealthy attachment.

One of the most subtle yet damaging symptoms in soul-tie entanglement is the habit of labeling emotional intensity as destiny. This symptom rarely announces itself as deception. Instead, it disguises itself as discernment. You tell yourself that the connection must have been meaningful because it felt powerful. You assume it must have been God-ordained because it awakened something deep inside you. You interpret the depth of the bond as proof of divine intent rather than evidence of emotional exposure.

This symptom often develops in people who are spiritually sincere. You pray. You seek God. You want to honor Him with your relationship. And because of that, you are especially vulnerable to mislabeling intensity as instruction. When a connection feels consuming, electric, or emotionally awakening, you begin to narrate it spiritually. You say things like, "I've never felt this way before," or "This has to mean something," or "God wouldn't let something feel this deep if it wasn't from Him."

Over time, this belief becomes a framework through which you interpret pain. Instead of questioning the health of the relationship, you question your endurance. Instead of evaluating alignment, you evaluate your faith. You tolerate confusion because you believe destiny is rarely comfortable. You dismiss inconsistency because you assume divine timing is mysterious. You spiritualize emotional chaos and call it growth.

This symptom is reinforced when the connection disrupts your peace but heightens your emotional awareness. You feel alive, alert, and deeply engaged, even while feeling anxious, unstable, or unsure. Because the experience feels transformative, you assume it must be sacred. But transformation alone does not equal covenant. Pain alone does not equal purpose.

What makes this symptom so persistent is how convincing it feels. Emotional intensity produces chemical responses in the brain that mimic significance. Dopamine and adrenaline amplify focus and attachment, making the connection feel urgent and irreplaceable. When these sensations are paired with spiritual language, they become almost impossible to question.

As a result, you remain tied to something that is draining you, not because it is good, but because you believe letting go would mean rejecting destiny itself.

TEACHING
Covenant produces peace. Soul ties produce intensity.

The difference between a soul tie and a covenant is not depth. It is direction. Covenant moves you forward in clarity. Soul ties pull you sideways into confusion. Covenant strengthens identity. Soul ties blur it. Covenant produces stability, even in difficulty. Soul ties produce emotional highs and lows that keep you off balance. God does not lead through chaos. He may stretch you, refine you, and challenge you, but He does not destabilize your sense of self in the name of purpose. When a relationship consistently disrupts your peace, compromises your boundaries, or requires you to abandon wisdom to maintain connection, it is not covenant. It is attachment. 

Covenant is not sustained by chemistry. It is sustained by commitment, accountability, and alignment. It does not require constant emotional reinforcement to survive. It does not rely on ambiguity to feel meaningful. Covenant is quiet, rooted, and consistent. It does not need to convince you of its legitimacy.

Soul ties, on the other hand, thrive on ambiguity. They feel intense because they are unstable. They keep you emotionally engaged because resolution is always just out of reach. They feel powerful because they activate survival mechanisms rather than security. God does not confuse His children to guide them. If a connection requires you to ignore wisdom, silence red flags, or spiritualize pain, it is not destiny. Destiny does not require self-betrayal.

Healing begins when you stop asking why the connection felt so deep and start asking whether it produced fruit that aligns with God's character. Destiny builds. Attachment consumption. Covenant covers. Soul ties cling. When you release the belief that intensity equals purpose, clarity begins to emerge. Peace returns not because the relationship was meaningless, but because you are no longer mislabeling it. God does not remove destiny. He removes confusion.

💊 Faith Prescription

Evaluating Alignment, Not Intensity

This week's prescription is truth-based evaluation. You are to stop assessing connections by how deeply they made you feel and start assessing them by how clearly, they allowed you to live. Reflect on whether the relationship strengthened your peace, identity, and obedience, or whether it required constant emotional negotiation. You are prescribed honesty without nostalgia. Do not revise the past to protect the attachment.

Dosage: Daily reflection. No spiritual justifications. No romantic rewriting.

🧬 Spiritual Vitamin

Wisdom Over Emotion

Your spiritual vitamin for this chapter is wisdom. Wisdom does not silence emotion; it contextualizes it.

Repeat daily: *"Depth without direction is not destiny."*

🕊 Holy Spirit Consult

Learning How God Actually Leads

Ask the Holy Spirit to retrain your discernment. Invite Him to show you the difference between emotional activation and divine confirmation. Ask Him to help you recognize peace as guidance, not boredom.

🙏 Guided Prayer

"God, forgive me for calling intensity destiny. Help me discern what is aligned versus what is merely emotional. Teach me to recognize covenant by its fruit, not its fire. I release every attachment that required confusion to survive. I receive clarity, wisdom, and peace. Amen."

📝 Journal Reflection Page

1. What did I interpret as destiny that was intensity?

____

____

____

____

____

2.	How did this connection affect my peace and identity?

____

____

____

____

3.	What red flags did I spiritualize instead of addressing?

____

____

____

____

4.	What would covenant-level peace feel like in my life?

____

____

____

____

Writing until truth feels steadier than emotion.

God does not disguise confusion as calling. Peace is the diagnostic marker of alignment.

☑ **NEXT APPOINTMENT**

PERSONAL NOTES

Chapter 7

"The Spiritual Cost Of Staying Too Long"

SYMPTOM
Gradual erosion of peace, clarity, and spiritual vitality caused by prolonged attachment to a misaligned relationship, often minimized because the damage happened slowly.

One of the most deceptive symptoms in soul-tie entanglement is not dramatic pain, but slow spiritual depletion. This symptom rarely shows up as a crisis. Instead, it arrives quietly, overtime, disguised as endurance, patience, loyalty, or faith. You do not wake up one day feeling completely disconnected from yourself or God. You drift there gradually. The change is subtle enough that you adapt without realizing what you are losing.

At first, staying feels noble. You believe you are being patient. You believe you are being loving. You believe you are honoring God by not giving up easily. You tolerate confusion because you assume clarity will come later. You excuse inconsistency because you believe growth takes time. You override your discomfort because you believe sacrifice is part of love. But slowly, something shifts inside you.

You begin to feel spiritually tired in ways rest does not fix. Prayer becomes harder to engage, not because you no longer believe, but because your inner world feels cluttered. Worship feels muted, not because God is distant, but because your attention is divided. Scripture feels less alive, not because it loses power, but because your heart is preoccupied with managing the relationship.

This symptom often shows up as internal compromise. You start ignoring small nudges. You delay obedience. You postpone decisions you know you need to make. You stop asking certain questions because you already know where the answers will lead.

You tell yourself that the discomfort is temporary, that God is still working, that you just need to hold on a little longer.

What you do not realize in the moment is that staying too long does not preserve the relationship, it reshapes you. You become less decisive. Less confident. Less anchored. You may notice that you no longer trust your discernment the way you used to. You second-guess yourself. You rely more heavily on the other person's responses to determine how you feel. Your peace becomes conditional. Your joy becomes delayed. Your sense of spiritual authority weakens, not because God removed it, but because you stopped exercising it.

This symptom is particularly difficult to detect because it does not feel like rebellion. It feels like restraint. It feels humility. It feels like waiting on God. But there is a difference between waiting in faith and stalling in fear. There is a difference between patience and postponement. There is a difference between endurance and disobedience.

Staying too long often costs you things you do not notice until they are gone clarity, confidence, emotional resilience, spiritual sharpness. By the time you recognize the cost, you may already feel depleted, confused, and disconnected from the version of yourself you used to be.

TEACHING
Delay in obedience always extracts a price.

God does not measure faithfulness by how long you endure misalignment. He measures it by how quickly you respond to truth. When God prompts movement and you delay it out of fear, attachment, or hope that circumstances will change, the delay itself becomes costly.

Staying too long in a misaligned relationship does not protect you from pain. It compounds it. Every day spent suppressing discernment strengthens the attachment while weakening your confidence. Over time, you begin to confuse exhaustion with maturity and depletion with devotion.

God never asks you to sacrifice your peace to prove your faith. Peace is not a reward for obedience; it is a guide for it. When peace consistently leaves a situation, it is not a test to see how long you can endure discomfort. It is information meant to prompt alignment. One of the hardest truths to accept is that God will allow you to stay where you are not meant to be, not because He approves, but because He honors your agency. He will continue to invite you forward, but He will not force you. The cost of staying becomes the teacher.

This is why spiritual dullness often accompanies prolonged misalignment. Not because God withdraws, but because attention is divided. You cannot fully engage God while constantly managing a relationship that requires emotional vigilance. Something always gets deprioritized, and it is usually your inner life.

Healing begins when you stop romanticizing endurance and start honoring obedience. Leaving late does not disqualify you, but it does require repair. The longer you stay past alignment, the more rebuilding is required afterward.

God is not angry that you stayed too long. He is patient. But patience does not erase consequences. Consequence is not punishment; it is feedback.

The good news is this: clarity returns quickly when alignment is restored. Peace resurfaces when attention is reclaimed. Spiritual vitality rebuilds when you stop spending it on what drains you. You did not lose yourself permanently. You overextended yourself temporarily. And restoration begins the moment you stop paying the cost.

Faith Prescription

Restoring What Was Slowly Drained

This week's prescription is restoration through honesty. You are prescribed reflection on what the relationship cost you spiritually and emotionally. Not to induce guilt, but to bring awareness. Naming the cost helps prevent repetition. You are also prescribed rest without explanation. You do not need to justify stepping back from what drained you.

Dosage: Daily reflection. Intentional rest. No minimizing the impact.

Spiritual Vitamin

Obedience Without Delay

Your spiritual vitamin for this chapter is responsiveness. Delayed obedience always feels safer than decisive obedience, but only one restores peace.

Repeat daily: *"I do not confuse endurance with obedience."*

Holy Spirit Consult

Rebuilding Spiritual Sensitivity

Ask the Holy Spirit to sharpen your discernment again. Invite Him to heal the places where you ignored His nudges out of fear or attachment. Ask Him to restore confidence in your ability to hear and respond.

🙏 Guided Prayer

"God, I acknowledge the cost of staying too long. I release guilt and receive responsibility. Restore what was drained while I delayed obedience. Teach me to trust You're leading without hesitation. I choose alignment over endurance. Amen."

📝 Journal Reflection Page

1. What did staying too long cost me emotionally or spiritually?

____

____

____

____

____

2. What nudges did I ignore, and why?

____

____

____

____

____

3. How has my peace changed since leaving?

____

---

4. What boundaries will I honor sooner next time? Write until clarity feels stronger than regret.

℞ Clinical Note

Endurance without alignment leads to depletion. Obedience restores strength.

☑ **NEXT APPOINTMENT**

PERSONAL NOTES

Chapter 8

"Why God Didn't Bless What He Didn't Assign"

SYMPTOM
Spiritual disappointment, confusion, and self-blame after investing deeply in a connection that never received the confirmation, fruit, or blessing you expected.

This symptom surfaces after you have done everything you know how to do spiritually, and the outcome still does not change. You prayed. You fasted. You sought counsel. You tried to be patient, faithful, and obedient. You asked God to bless the relationship, to heal it, to fix what felt broken, and to bring clarity where confusion persisted. Instead of confirmation, you encountered resistance. Instead of fruit, you experienced frustration. And instead of peace, you felt increasingly unsettled.

What makes this symptom particularly painful is the belief that spiritual effort should guarantee spiritual results. When blessing does not follow investment, you begin to question yourself. You wonder whether your faith was insufficient, whether you misunderstood God, or whether you somehow blocked His blessing through personal failure. Disappointment quietly turns inward, and self-blame begins to grow.

This symptom often shows up as spiritual bargaining. You replay prayers and promise in your mind. You ask yourself whether you prayed the wrong way or missed a step. You may even feel embarrassed to admit how much hope you placed in something that never aligned. Over time, disappointment hardens into confusion, and confusion erodes trust—not just in relationships, but in your own discernment.

Emotionally, you feel let down. Spiritually, you feel misled. And internally, you feel torn between honoring God and mourning something that never became what you believed it could be. You may wrestle with the question, *"If God is good, why didn't He bless this?"* What you may not realize yet is that the absence of blessing was not punishment, it was protection.

TEACHING
God does not bless attachments He did not assign.

One of the hardest truths to accept in healing is that God's silence or resistance is often an answer, not an absence. God blesses what He assigns, not what we insist on sustaining. When something is misaligned, no amount of prayer can convert attachment into assignment. Spiritual effort cannot override divine wisdom.

God's blessing is not transactional. It is directional. He blesses what leads you forward in purpose, not what keeps you emotionally stuck. When a connection consistently disrupts your peace, blurs your identity, or requires you to compromise discernment, the absence of blessing is not cruel, it is clarity. Many people confuse blessing with endurance. They assume that if they can just hold on long enough, God will eventually confirm what they desire. But confirmation is not produced by persistence. It is revealed through alignment. God does not withhold blessing to test your loyalty. He withholds it to prevent harm.

When you stop blaming yourself for the absence of blessing, healing accelerates. You begin to see that unanswered prayers were not rejections, they were redirections. God was not ignoring you. He was guarding you from building a future on something temporary.

This realization can feel sobering, even painful. It requires you to grieve not just the relationship, but the future you imagined. Yet within that grief is freedom. When you accept that God did not assign the connection, you are released from trying to fix it. You are no longer responsible for making it work. You are free to let go without guilt. God does not remove what He intends to bless. He removes what He intends to replace. When you release the belief that blessing was withheld because of failure, peace begins to return. You stop striving. You stop bargaining. You stop asking God to endorse something He already protected you from. And clarity settles in its place.

✏ Faith Prescription

Releasing The Need For Divine Approval

This week's prescription is surrendered without negotiation. You are prescribed acceptance that God's lack of blessing was an act of mercy. Stop trying to spiritualize what was never assigned. You are also prescribed forgiveness, toward yourself, for believing in something that did not align.

Dosage: Daily release. No spiritual bargaining. No self-blame.

Spiritual Vitamin

Trust Over Understanding

Your spiritual vitamin for this chapter is trust. God's protection often feels like disappointment before it feels like freedom.
Repeat daily: *"God protects me through redirection."*

Holy Spirit Consult

Seeing Silence as Safety

Ask the Holy Spirit to reframe unanswered prayers. Invite Him to replace confusion with understanding and disappointment with peace. Ask Him to help you trust His restraint.

🙏 Guided Prayer

"God, I release my need to understand every unanswered prayer. I trust that Your lack of blessing was not rejection, but protection. Heal the disappointment I carried and restore my confidence in Your leading. I choose peace over explanation. Amen."

📝 Journal Reflection Page

1. What prayers went unanswered, and how did I interpret that?

____

____

____

____

____

2. How did I internalize the absence of blessing?

____

____

____

____

____

3. What future did I grieve for that never became reality?

____

____

____

4. How does it change things to see redirection as protection?

Write until relief replaces resistance.

⚕ Clinical Note

God's silence is not neglect. It is often safety.

☑ **NEXT APPOINTMENT**

PART III:
THE TREATMENT PLAN

PERSONAL NOTES

Chapter 9

"You Can't Heal While Still Feeding The Tie"

SYMPTOM
Repeated emotional setbacks caused by continued behaviors that reinforce attachment, even after the relationship has ended.

One of the most frustrating symptoms in the healing process is the feeling that you are doing everything right, yet nothing seems to change. You have accepted that the relationship is over. You have acknowledged that it was not aligned. You have prayed, reflected, and committed to moving forward. And still, the attachment feels stubbornly alive. Peace flickers in and out. Progress feels inconsistent. You find yourself asking why healing feels slower than expected.

This symptom often reveals itself through subtle behaviors that keep the soul tie nourished. You may not be in contact with the person, but you still check their social media. You may not speak to them directly, but you replay memories, conversations, or imagined scenarios in your mind. You may not want them back, but you still hold space for them emotionally wondering how they are, what they think of you, or whether they miss you.

What makes this symptom especially deceptive is that none of these behaviors feel dramatic. They feel harmless. They feel private. They feel justified. You tell yourself that you are just processing, just reflecting, just being human. But healing cannot fully take root while the attachment is still being fed, even in small, invisible ways.

This symptom often shows emotional confusion. Some days you feel strong and resolved. Other days you feel pulled backward without understanding why. You may interpret this inconsistency as weakness or lack of discipline, when it is the natural result of ***mixed signals*** being sent to your nervous system. Part of you is letting go. Another part of you is still holding on.

Feeding the tie does not always look like contact. It often looks like fantasy. It looks like nostalgia without context. It looks like replaying what was instead of grounding yourself in what is. Each time you engage in these behaviors, you reinforce the attachment, even as you consciously desire freedom from it.

Spiritually, this symptom can be confusing. You may ask God to heal you while simultaneously revisiting the wound. You may pray for peace while mentally reopening doors you asked Him to close. This inner contradiction delays healing, not because God withholds it, but because your system is receiving conflicting instructions. You are not failing at healing. You are feeding what you are trying to release. And healing cannot coexist with reinforcement.

TEACHING
Healing requires both surrender and discipline.

Letting go is not a single decision. It is a series of consistent choices that retrain your inner world. When a soul tie forms, it creates emotional, mental, and sometimes spiritual habits. Those habits do not dissolve through insight alone. They dissolve through interruption.

God's role in healing is to provide truth, grace, and strength. Your role is to cooperate with the process. Cooperation looks like removing access, not just physically, but emotionally and mentally. Healing accelerates when you stop giving your attention to what no longer belongs in your future.

Feeding a soul tie keeps it alive. Attention is nourishment. Emotional engagement is reinforcement. When you revisit memories without grounding them in truth, you keep the attachment warm. When you allow fantasy to replace reality, you strengthen longing. When you avoid boredom or loneliness by revisiting the past, you delay restoration.

God does not shame you for struggling with this. He understands that attachment dissolves gradually. But He does call you into responsibility. Healing deepens when you choose alignment over comfort and discipline overindulgence.

This is why boundaries are not punishment. They are medicine. Boundaries protect healing while it is still fragile. They create space for new patterns to form. They reduce stimulation so your nervous system can reset. You cannot heal while still feeding the tie because healing requires starvation of the attachment and nourishment of the self. As you reduce reinforcement, peace slowly stabilizes. As you redirect energy, identity strengthens. As you practice discipline, freedom expands.

This chapter is not about perfection. It is about honesty. Healing does not require you to never think about them again. It requires you to stop *returning* to them emotionally. Freedom begins when you stop feeding what keeps your bond.

💊 Faith Prescription

Interrupting Attachment Reinforcement

This week's prescription is intentional interruption. You are to identify the behaviors, mental, emotional, or digital, that keep the soul tie active and consciously interrupt them. This is not about self-control through shame. It is about protection through awareness. You are prescribed redirection. When the urge to revisit the past arises, redirect your attention to the present moment or to an activity that grounds you in your body and your life now.

Dosage: Daily awareness. Immediate redirection. No nostalgic indulgence.

✿ Spiritual Vitamin

Discipline as Compassion

Your spiritual vitamin for this chapter is discipline. Discipline is not harsh. It is compassion for your future self.

Repeat daily: *"I do not feed what keeps me bound."*

🕊 Holy Spirit Consult

Strengthening Self-Leadership

Invite the Holy Spirit to strengthen your ability to lead yourself through discomfort. Ask Him to help you recognize when you are feeding attachment and to give you the strength to choose differently.

🙏 Guided Prayer

"God, I acknowledge the ways I have fed attachments while asking You to heal them. I release habits that keep me emotionally tethered to the past. Teach me discipline without shame and awareness without fear. I choose freedom, even when it requires restraint. Amen."

📝 Journal Reflection Page

1. What behaviors keep the soul tie active in my life?

____

____

____

____

____

2.   When do I feel most tempted to revisit the past?

____

____

____

____

3.   What emotions am I avoiding by feeding the attachment?

____

____

____

____

4.   What new habits can nourish my healing instead?

____

____

____

____

Write until intention replaces impulse.

⚕ Clinical Note

You cannot starve an attachment you keep feeding. Discipline protects healing.

☑ **NEXT APPOINTMENT**

PERSONAL NOTES

Chapter 10
"The Detox Season Nobody Celebrates"

SYMPTOM

Emotional emptiness, loneliness, irritability, and grief that surface after cutting off attachment, often mistaken for regression or proof that healing was a mistake.

There is a moment in healing that almost no one prepares you for, the moment when you finally stop feeding the tie, and instead of immediate relief, you feel empty. Not dramatic emptiness. Not despair. Just a quiet, hollow absence where something used to live. The noise is gone. Chaos has settled. And instead of peace rushing in like a reward, silence fills the space. This is the detox season.

This symptom feels unsettling because it contradicts expectation. You assumed that once you stopped checking, stopped reaching, stopped replaying, and stopped hoping, you would feel lighter. You feel exposed. You notice the quiet more than the freedom. You feel the absence more than the relief. And you begin to wonder whether letting go makes things worse.

This symptom often presents as loneliness that feels sharper than before. Not because you are alone, but because the emotional stimulation that once distracted you is gone. You are no longer busy managing someone else's moods, interpreting mixed signals, or sustaining hope that things will change. Without that activity, your inner world feels still, and stillness can feel threatening when you are not used to it. You may also feel emotionally irritable. Small things bother you. Your patience feels thin. You may feel restless, bored, or unsettled without knowing why. This does not mean healing is failing. It means your nervous system is recalibrating after prolonged stimulation.

Another part of this symptom is grief that feels confusing because you have already decided to leave. You may think, *"Why am I grieving something I know wasn't right?"* But grief does not only come from losing something good. It comes from losing something familiar. It comes from releasing a pattern that once helped you cope, even if it harmed you long-term.

Spiritually, this season can feel flat. Prayers may feel quiet. Worship may feel less emotional. You may interpret this as spiritual dryness when it is emotional detox. Your soul is learning how to exist without the highs and lows that once defined connection.

This symptom is dangerous only when misunderstood. When people misinterpret detox as regression, they often reattach, not because they want the relationship back, but because they want the discomfort to stop. Detox discomfort tempts you to romanticize the past simply to escape the present. But this emptiness is not a void meant to be refilled quickly. It is space meant to be *respected*.

TEACHING
Detox is not loss. It is transition.

Every meaningful healing process includes a detox phase. Detox happens when the source of stimulation is removed and the body, mind, and soul must relearn how to regulate without it. In physical healing, detox is expected. In emotional healing, it is often feared and misinterpreted.

The discomfort you feel in this season is not proof that you need what you let go of. It is proof that your system is adapting. Emotional attachment releases chemicals that affect mood, motivation, and focus. When that stimulation is removed, your system temporarily feels unbalanced. This is not spiritual failure. It is biological and emotional recalibration.

God does not rush to refill the space left by unhealthy attachment because premature filling prevents proper healing. If something immediately replaces what you released, the deeper work never happens. Detox creates space for identity to resurface, for desires to clarify, and for peace to return without dependency.

This is why God often feels quieter in detox seasons. He is not absent. He is allowing your soul to settle. He is teaching you how to exist without constant emotional noise. Peace that comes after detox is different from peace that comes through relief. It is sturdier. Quieter. Less reactive.

Detox also exposes truths you could not see while attached. In the quiet, you begin to recognize how much energy you were expending to maintain the bond. You see how much of yourself was oriented around someone else. This awareness can feel painful, but it is also empowering. You are not broken, you were overextended.

This season requires patience. Not endurance for pain, but respect for process. Detox cannot be rushed without consequence. If you try to bypass it through distraction, replacement relationships, or constant stimulation, the attachment simply transfers instead of dissolving. God does not abandon you in detox. He stabilizes you there. The emptiness you feel is not a problem to solve. It is a transition to honor.

💊 Faith Prescription

Staying Present Through Detox

This week's prescription is presence. You are prescribed to stay with yourself without rushing to fill space. When loneliness or emptiness arises, I acknowledge it without labeling it as failure. Let it pass without panic.
You are also prescribed simplicity. Reduce unnecessary stimulation. Allow your system to rest.

Dosage: Daily stillness. No replacement attachments. No forced positivity.

🧬 Spiritual Vitamin

Trusting the In-Between

Your spiritual vitamin for this chapter is trust. Trust that God is working in the quiet. Trust that this season has purpose.

Repeat daily: *"This emptiness is not permanent. It is preparing me."*

🕊 Holy Spirit Consult

Learning To Be With Yourself

Ask the Holy Spirit to help you feel safe in stillness. Invite Him to comfort you without distraction and to teach you how to rest without escape.

🙏 Guided Prayer

"God, I acknowledge the emptiness I feel now that I've let go. Help me resist the urge to refill this space prematurely. Teach me how to sit with myself and trust that You are restoring me in the quiet. I choose patience over panic. Amen."

📝 Journal Reflection Page

1. What emotions surface when the noise is gone?

____

____

____

2. What did the attachment distract me from feeling?

3. What do I fear will happen if I stay in this quiet?

4. What might God be rebuilding in this space?

Write until stillness feels safer than distraction.

⚕ Clinical Note

Detoxes feel like emptiness before it feels like freedom. Do not interrupt the process.

☑ **NEXT APPOINTMENT**

Chapter 11

"Learning To Sit With The Void Without Refilling It"

SYMPTOM

Anxious urgency to replace what was lost, accompanied by discomfort with stillness, silence, and emotional space.

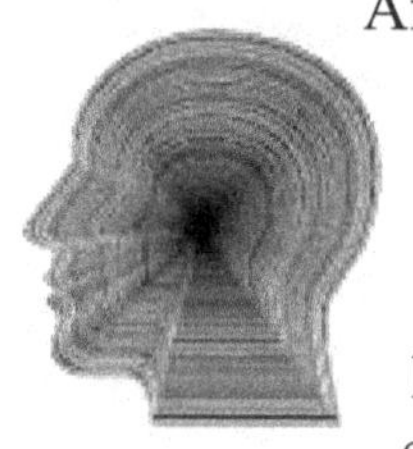

After the initial shock of detox settles, a new symptom often emerges, one that is quieter but just as powerful. You are no longer actively attached, but you are deeply uncomfortable with the space left behind. The chaos is gone. The noise has faded. And now there is a void. Not dramatic emptiness. Not despair. Just space. Too much space.

This symptom shows up as restlessness. You feel an almost physical urge to *do something,* to talk to someone, to scroll, to date, to distract, to plan, to stay busy. Stillness feels unsafe. Silence feels suspicious. You tell yourself you are bored, but what you are experiencing is unfamiliar peace without structure.

The void feels wrong because your system was trained to associate connection with stimulation. When that stimulation is gone, your nervous system searches for replacement. Not necessarily because you want another relationship, but because your identity has not yet re-centered around yourself.

You may notice yourself fantasizing about future connections prematurely. You may romanticize the idea of "someone new" not out of readiness, but out of discomfort with being alone. You may overcommit socially, spiritually, or professionally just to avoid being still. None of this means you are regressing. It means you are standing at the edge of real healing.

This symptom becomes dangerous when the void is treated like a problem instead of a passage. When people rush to refill it, they often choose familiarity over alignment. They attach before discerning. They replace them before healing. And the cycle repeats, not because they failed, but because they never learned how to sit with space long enough for clarity to form. The void is not empty. It is unclaimed.

TEACHING
The void is where identity is rebuilt.

God often removes attachment before He reveals direction. This space between what was and what will be is not accidental. It is intentional. The void exists so you can return to yourself without interference. It is where misplaced identity is reclaimed. When you rush to refill the void, you rob yourself of discernment.

You do not yet know what you truly want, what you truly need, or who you truly are outside of the attachment. Stillness gives those answers room to surface. God is not in a hurry to replace what He removed. He is far more interested in restoring you than assigning someone new. If the void feels uncomfortable, it is because you are no longer being distracted from yourself.

Learning to sit with the void requires courage. It requires you to resist urgency. It requires you to trust that space is not abandoned. It requires you to believe that peace does not need noise to exist.

Healing deepens when you allow the void to remain unfilled until clarity arrives naturally. Over time, the space becomes less threatening. You begin to enjoy your own presence. You begin to recognize your desires without external influence. You begin to feel grounded without attachment. This is not loneliness. This is **integration**. The void teaches you that you are not incomplete. You were interrupted.

💊 Faith Prescription

Practicing Stillness Without Replacement

This week's prescription is intentional stillness. You are to resist filling space with new attachments, constant activity, or emotional substitutes. When discomfort arises, sit with it instead of escaping it. You are prescribed patience with the unknown.

Dosage: Daily quiet time. No premature connections. No impulsive decisions.

🧬 Spiritual Vitamin

Comfort with Self

Your spiritual vitamin for this chapter is self-comfort. Learn to be safe in your own presence.

Repeat daily: *"I do not rush what God is restoring."*

🕊 Holy Spirit Consult

Receiving Direction Without Urgency

Ask the Holy Spirit to teach you how to wait without anxiety. Invite Him to replace urgency with trust and restlessness with assurance.

🙏 Guided Prayer

"God, I resist the urge to refill the space You created. Teach me how to be still without fear. Help me trust that You are rebuilding me in this season. I choose patience over urgency. Amen."

 Journal Reflection Page

1. What do I feel tempted to replace quickly?

____

____

____

____

2. What does stillness reveal about me?

____

____

____

____

3. What fears surface when I sit with the void?

____

____

____

____

4. How might this space be preparing me for something healthier?

____

____

____

____

____

Write until peace feels familiar.

🩺 Clinical Note

Do not rush to refill what God intentionally emptied. The void is sacred space.

☑ **NEXT APPOINTMENT**

PERSONAL NOTES

____

____

____

____

____

____

____

____

____

____

____

____

____

Chapter 12

"Forgiveness Is Not Reattachment"

SYMPTOM

Confusion between forgiveness and access, often resulting in reopened communication, emotional re-entanglement, or renewed obligation disguised as spiritual maturity.

One of the most misleading symptoms in the healing process appears right when you believe you are doing something spiritually right. You feel convicted to forgive. You recognize that holding resentment is heavy. You genuinely want to be free, not bitter. And because forgiveness is preached as essential to healing, you assume it must include restoration of access. You tell yourself that if you were truly healed, you would not need distance. You would not feel guarded. You would not hesitate to reconnect.

This symptom often shows up as spiritual pressure. You feel compelled to reach out "in peace." You consider reopening communication to prove you are no longer affected. You may even believe that refusing access means you have not forgiven. The desire to appear spiritually mature overrides your need for emotional safety.

When forgiveness becomes confused with reattachment, healing stalls. You reopen emotional doors under the guise of grace. You allow conversations that stir old feelings. You re-enter dynamics that once destabilized you, believing that maturity requires proximity.

This symptom is especially dangerous in faith spaces where forgiveness is emphasized without equal emphasis on boundaries. You are taught to release offense, but not how to protect healing. You are encouraged to love freely but not taught how to love wisely. Over time, you internalize the belief that distance is unchristian and that access is proof of forgiveness.

What you may not realize is that forgiveness is an internal act, not an external invitation. Forgiveness changes your posture toward someone, not your boundaries around them. When you confuse forgiveness with access, you place your healing back into someone else's hands.

This symptom often leads to emotional regression. After reattaching, even briefly, you notice familiar reactions returning. You feel unsettled. You question your clarity. You feel drawn back into patterns you thought were resolved. And shame follows, because you believed forgiveness would feel cleaner than this. But forgiveness was never meant to reopen wounds. It was meant to close them.

TEACHING
Forgiveness releases debt: boundaries protect peace.

Forgiveness is one of the most misunderstood spiritual practices, especially in the context of emotional healing. Forgiveness does not require reconciliation. It does not require access. It does not require explanation. It requires release. When Jesus spoke about forgiveness, He addressed the condition of the heart, not the structure of the relationship. Forgiveness removes bitterness so it no longer poisons you. Boundaries remove access so harm cannot continue.

God does not confuse forgiveness with trust. Trust is built through consistent behavior over time. Forgiveness can happen instantly. Trust cannot. When you restore access without evidence of change, you are not practicing grace, you are abandoning discernment.

Forgiveness is powerful because it breaks emotional bondage. Reattachment rebuilds it. Healing deepens when forgiveness happens privately and boundaries remain intact publicly. You are allowed to forgive someone and still choose distance. You are allowed to release resentment and still say no. You are allowed to wish someone well without re-entering their life. These are not contradictions. They are signs of maturity. God does not require you to place yourself back in harm's way to prove your heart is clean. He values your peace. He honors wisdom. He protects healing.

Forgiveness frees you from the past. Boundaries protect your future. When you stop equating forgiveness with access, peace stabilizes. You stop feeling guilty for choosing distance. You stop negotiating with yourself. You stop reopening emotional doors you worked hard to close. Healing is not proven by proximity. It is proven by peace.

💊 Faith Prescription

Forgive Without Reopening Access

This week's prescription is forgiveness without proximity. You are prescribed internal release paired with external boundaries. You are not required to announce forgiveness or demonstrate it through access. You are also prescribed clarity. Forgiveness is complete when resentment no longer controls you, not when contact resumes.

Dosage: One intentional release prayer. Ongoing boundary reinforcement. No guilt-based access.

🧬 Spiritual Vitamin

Wisdom with Compassion

Your spiritual vitamin for this chapter is wisdom. Wisdom allows compassion without self-betrayal.

Repeat daily: *"I forgive without reopening doors."*

🕊 Holy Spirit Consult

Separating Grace from Access

Ask the Holy Spirit to help you distinguish grace from availability. Invite Him to strengthen your boundaries and remove guilt associated with distance.

🙏 Guided Prayer

"God, I release resentment without reopening access. I forgive myself without placing myself back in harm's way. Teach me how to honor healing without guilt. I trust You to handle what I no longer carry. Amen."

📝 Journal Reflection Page

1. Where have I confused forgiveness with access?

____

____

____

____

2. What guilt do I feel about maintaining distance?

____

____

____

____

3. How has reattachment affected my peace in the past?

____

____

____

____

4. What boundaries protect my healing now?

____

____

____

____

____

____

____

____

____

____

Write until freedom feels stable.

⚕ Clinical Note

Forgiveness heals the heart. Boundaries protect the soul.
☑ **NEXT APPOINTMENT**

PART IV:
THE RECOVERY PLAN

PERSONAL NOTES

Chapter 13

"When Healing Feels Like Losing Part Of Yourself"

SYMPTOM

A deep sense of identity loss, grief, and disorientation after detaching from a soul tie, often described as feeling empty, unfamiliar to oneself, or unsure who you are without the connection.

There is a specific kind of grief that appears only after real healing begins. It is not the grief of missing the person. It is the grief of missing who you were while connected to them. This symptom can be unsettling because it does not feel like heartbreak, it feels like dislocation. You wake up and realize that parts of your identity were quietly organized around someone else, and now those reference points are gone. You may feel unsure of yourself in small but persistent ways. Decisions feel heavier. Preferences feel unclear. Even joy can feel unfamiliar, not because it is absent, but because it is no longer shared, mirrored, or validated by another person. You may catch yourself thinking, *"I don't recognize myself anymore,"* and feel alarmed by that thought.

This symptom is especially painful because it feels like a loss you cannot explain to others. People may tell you that you should feel stronger, freer, or more empowered now that the attachment is gone. Instead, you feel quieter. Less defined. Less certain. Healing feels less like victory and more like mourning.

What is happening is identity withdrawal. When a soul tie forms, identity subtly shifts. You adapt. You adjust. You prioritize. Over time, your sense of self becomes partially relational rather than internal. When that relationship ends, the self that was shaped around it dissolves. This does not mean you lose yourself permanently. It means you outgrew a version of yourself that was built around survival, accommodation, or emotional proximity.

This symptom often brings fear. You may worry that you will never feel whole again, that something essential was taken from you, or that healing required too much sacrifice. You may question whether the cost of peace was worth it. These thoughts are not evidence of regression. They are evidence of transition. You are not losing yourself. You are meeting yourself without attachments.

TEACHING
Healing removes borrowed identity so identity can surface.

God does not heal by amputating who you are. He heals by removing what was never meant to define you. When healing feels like loss, it is often because identity was built in layers, some of which were formed in response to another person rather than in alignment with your core self.

The disorientation you feel is not emptiness. It is integration in progress. This season invites you to ask different questions, not "Who was I to them?" but "Who am I becoming now?" Identity formed in attachment feels familiar, but identity formed in wholeness feels quieter at first. It does not rely on affirmation, proximity, or intensity to feel real.

God rebuilds identity from the inside out. He restores clarity before confidence. He restores grounding before momentum. That process can feel slow, but it is stable. This is why rushing into new roles, new relationships, or new labels can delay recovery. Identity needs space to settle. It needs stillness to recalibrate. When you allow this process to unfold naturally, something surprising happens you begin to enjoy your own company again. You recognize preferences that were muted. You feel strength where you once felt dependence.

Healing did not take something from you. It returned to you. The grief you feel is not for who you lost. It is for who you no longer need to be.

🔖 Faith Prescription

Reclaiming Identity Without Replacement

This week's prescription is self-reintroduction. You are prescribed time alone without self-judgment. Explore who you are now without trying to label it too quickly. Let curiosity replace pressure. You are also prescribed gentleness. Identity restoration is not rushed.

Dosage: Daily self-check-in. No identity substitutions. No performance-based healing.

🧬 Spiritual Vitamin

Wholeness Over Familiarity

Your spiritual vitamin for this chapter is wholeness. Familiarity feels safe, but wholeness is stable.

Repeat daily: *"I am not losing myself. I am returning to myself."*

🕊 Holy Spirit Consult

Letting God Define You Again

Ask the Holy Spirit to reveal who you are apart from attachment. Invite Him to rebuild identity without pressure, fear, or comparison.

🙏 Guided Prayer

"God, I bring You the grief of becoming someone new. Help me trust this process of rediscovery. Restore my identity without urgency and my confidence without attachment. I receive who I am becoming. Amen."

📝 Journal Reflection Page

1. Who was I while attached to that I no longer need to be?

____

____

____

____

____

____

____

2. What parts of myself feel unfamiliar right now?

____

____

____

3. What do I enjoy without needing to share it?

____

____

____

4. How might this season be redefining me in healthy ways?

____

____

____

Write until curiosity replaces fear.

⚕ Clinical Note

Healing feels like loss when identity is borrowed. Wholeness restores what attachment is redefined.

☑ NEXT APPOINTMENT

PERSONAL NOTES

Chapter 14

"Relearning Joy Without Emotional Crutches"

SYMPTOM

A muted sense of joy, difficulty experiencing pleasure without emotional reinforcement, and discomfort enjoying life independently after detaching from a soul tie.

One of the quieter but most unsettling symptoms in recovery appears when the chaos finally subsides and you expect joy to return, yet it doesn't arrive the way you imagined. Life looks calmer. Your decisions feel cleaner. Your boundaries are stronger. And still, joy feels distant. Not absent, just... muted. You laugh, but it feels shallow. You enjoy moments, but they don't linger. Happiness shows up briefly, then fades without explanation.

This symptom is confusing because it contradicts the narrative you were told about healing. You assumed that once the attachment ended and peace stabilized, joy would rush in and fill the space. Instead, joy feels cautious. Reserved. Almost shy. You begin to wonder whether something is wrong with you, whether healing somehow dulled your emotional capacity, or whether joy was tied to the intensity you released.

What is happening is emotional recalibration. For a long time, your nervous system associated joy with stimulation. Excitement was paired with unpredictability. Pleasure was tied to anticipation, affirmation, or emotional highs that came from someone else's presence. When that stimulation is removed, your system does not immediately recognize quieter forms of joy as meaningful. Peace feels unfamiliar. Stability feels uneventful. Joy without intensity feels underwhelming, not because it lacks depth, but because it lacks drama.

This symptom often leads to subtle self-doubt. You may wonder whether healing makes you less passionate or less alive. You may miss the emotional spikes, even if you do not miss the pain. You may feel tempted to seek excitement through distraction, busyness, or premature connections, not because you want chaos back, but because you want to feel something *strong* again.

This is the danger point. Not to relapse into attachment, but relapse into emotional dependence on stimulation. Joy has not disappeared. It has changed forms.

TEACHING
Joy that survives healing is quieter, but deeper.

Joy rooted in attachment is reactive. It depends on response, affirmation, and proximity. Joy rooted in wholeness is internal. It does not need reinforcement to exist. It does not rise and fall with someone else's availability. It is steadier, slower, and far more sustainable. God does not remove joy when He removes attachments. He **redefines** it. 

The transition from attachment-based joy to wholeness-based joy requires patience. Your nervous system must learn to recognize calm as safety and stability as satisfaction. This learning does not happen overnight. It happens through repetition, by allowing yourself to enjoy moments without amplifying them, posting them, sharing them, or tying them to someone else's reaction.

Joy begins to return when you stop searching for intensity and start noticing contentment. It appears in small ways: finishing a day without emotional exhaustion, enjoying a quiet morning, laughing without needing to explain why. These moments may feel insignificant at first, but they are signs of deep healing. God is not interested in giving you joy that requires emotional crutches to survive. He is building joy that stands on his own. Joy remains even when no one is watching. Joy that does not disappear when circumstances shift.

Relearning joy means allowing pleasure without guilt and calm without suspicion. It means trusting that excitement does not have to come with anxiety to be real. It means believing that joy does not need chaos to feel meaningful. This kind of joy does not rush in. It settles. And when it settles, it stays.

Faith Prescription

Allowing Joy To Be Gentle

This week's prescription is gentle enjoyment. You are prescribed permission to enjoy moments without amplifying them or attaching meaning to them. Let joy be small. Let it be quiet. Let it be enough. You are also prescribed patience. Joy is returning to a healthier pace.

Dosage: Daily enjoyment of one simple moment. No comparison to past highs No pressure to feel more.

Spiritual Vitamin

Contentment Without Stimulation

Your spiritual vitamin for this chapter is contentment. Contentment is not boredom. It is stability.

Repeat daily: *"Joy does not need intensity to be real."*

Holy Spirit Consult

Recognizing Joy in New Forms

Ask the Holy Spirit to help you recognize joy without needing it to look like the past. Invite Him to attune your heart to peace-based pleasure.

🙏 Guided Prayer

"God, teach me how to receive joy without chaos. Help me trust joy that is calm, steady, and quiet. Retrain my heart to recognize peace as pleasure. I receive joy that lasts. Amen."

📝 Journal Reflection Page

1. How has my understanding of joy changed since healing began?

____

____

____

____

2. What simple moments bring me peace now?

____

____

____

____

3. Where do I feel tempted to chase intensity?

____

____

____

____

4. What would it look like to let joy arrive slowly?

____

____

____

____

Write until gratitude replaces longing.

🩺 Clinical Note

Joy rooted in wholeness does not scream. It stays.

☑ **NEXT APPOINTMENT**

PERSONAL NOTES

____

____

____

____

____

____

____

____

____

____

____

____

PART V: AFTERCARE

PERSONAL NOTES

Chapter 15

"Why Familiar Feels Safe But Isn't Always Holy"

SYMPTOM

A persistent pull toward familiar patterns, people, and dynamics after healing, often mistaken for discernment, comfort, or God's peace.

After real healing takes root and life begins to stabilize, a subtle but powerful symptom often emerges familiarity starts calling your name. Not loudly. Not urgently. Gently. Comfortably. You find yourself drawn toward what you already knew, familiar personalities, predictable dynamics, even when those things previously disrupt your peace.

This symptom is dangerous because it does not feel like temptation. It feels reasonable. Familiarity offers predictability, and predictability feels safe to a nervous system that spends a long time in instability. You tell yourself that you are just being cautious, grounded, or discerning. Your system is scanning for what it recognizes, not what is healthy.

You may notice thoughts like, *"At least I know what to expect,"* or *"This feels normal,"* or *"I don't want to start from scratch."* Familiarity lowers your guard. It softens your boundaries. It makes you more willing to tolerate small compromises because the terrain feels known.

This symptom often shows up after progress, not during crisis. When peace becomes consistent, boredom or restlessness can creep in. You may begin to miss the emotional engagement that once made you feel alive. Not the pain, but the familiarity of navigating it. Your system confuses stimulation with safety and repetition with righteousness.

Spiritually, this symptom can masquerade as peace. You may interpret the absence of anxiety around familiar dynamics as God's approval. But comfort is not confirmation. Just because something no longer alarms you does not mean it aligns with where you are now. Familiarity does not ask permission to return. It waits for vulnerability.

TEACHING
Familiarity feels safe because it is known, not because it is good.

The human nervous system is wired to seek what it recognizes. Familiarity reduces cognitive load. It requires less adjustment. It feels efficient. But healing changes your capacity, not you're wiring. Even after growth, your system will still gravitate toward what it knows unless consciously redirected. God does not lead through familiarity alone.

He leads through fruit, alignment, and peace that deepens, not peace that simply feels predictable. When healing has done its work, familiar dynamics often feel comfortable because your tolerance has increased, not because the dynamic has improved. This is why discernment must be intentional after healing. You can no longer rely on comfort as a guide.

You must evaluate whether a connection honors who you are now, not who you used to be. God does not sanctify what He already healed you from. He invites you forward, not backward. Familiarity that pulls you into old patterns is not holy, it is habitual.

Aftercare requires vigilance without fear. You are not guarding against people; you are guarding your peace. You are not resisting connection; you are refining it. Healing matures when you choose alignment over recognition. Familiarity asks, *"Does this feel known?"* Wisdom asks, *"Does this bear fruit?"*

💊 Faith Prescription

Evaluating Safety Through Fruit, Not Familiarity

This week's prescription is conscious evaluation. You are prescribed slowing down when familiarity feels appealing. Ask whether the connection supports growth, peace, and integrity. You are also prescribed curiosity over compliance.

Dosage: Pause before engagement. Assess patterns honestly. No nostalgia-driven decisions.

🧬 Spiritual Vitamin

Discernment Beyond Comfort

Your spiritual vitamin for this chapter is discernment. Discernment protects healing when comfort tries to override wisdom.
Repeat daily: *"Comfort is not my compass."*

🕊 Holy Spirit Consult

Learning to Discern Forward

Ask the Holy Spirit to sharpen your awareness of patterns. Invite Him to help you recognize what belongs to your future rather than what feels familiar from your past.

🙏 Guided Prayer

"God, help me resist the pull of familiarity when it does not align with who I am becoming. Teach me to evaluate connections by fruit, not comfort. Guard my peace and refine my discernment. Amen."

📝 Journal Reflection Page

1. What familiar patterns feel tempting right now?

____

____

____

____

2. How did familiarity keep me bound in the past?

____

____

____

____

3. What fruit do I want future connections to produce?

____

____

____

____

4. What boundaries protect my healing today?

____

____

____

____

Write until wisdom feels stronger than comfort.

⚕ Clinical Note

Familiarity does not mean safety. Healing requires discernment, not nostalgia.

☑ **NEXT APPOINTMENT**

PERSONAL NOTES

Chapter 16
"Discernment Is Not Bitterness"

SYMPTOM

Fear of appearing hardened, unforgiving, or emotionally closed after healing, often leading to self-doubt, boundary erosion, or overcorrection in relationships

After you have done real healing work, something strange can happen. You become clearer. Quieter. Less reactive. You notice red flags sooner. You ask better questions. You feel less compelled to explain yourself. And instead of feeling proud of that growth, you begin to worry that something is wrong with you. You may wonder whether healing has made you cold. You question whether your boundaries are walls. You ask yourself if you have become bitter, guarded, or emotionally unavailable. When you hesitate to engage with someone new, you wonder if fear is masquerading as wisdom. When you say no without guilt, you worry that compassion has been replaced by indifference.

This symptom is especially common among people who were once deeply accommodated. When your identity is shaped around empathy, availability, or emotional labor, discernment can feel unfamiliar. You are no longer moved by emergency. You no longer rush to fix, rescue, or reassure. And because this version of you feels different, it can feel wrong.

Others may reinforce this confusion. People accustomed to your access may label your boundaries as distance. Those who benefited from your over-giving may accuse you of changing. You may hear things like, *"You're different now,"* or *"You don't open up like you used to."* And part of you wonder if they are right.

This symptom can lead to overcorrection. You soften boundaries prematurely to prove you are still loving. You tolerate discomfort to avoid being seen as rigid. You second-guess instincts that once protected you. In trying not to become bitter, you risk becoming unprotected. What you are experiencing is not bitterness.

It is discernment activating after healing. Bitterness hardens the heart. Discernment clarifies it. Bitterness isolates. Discernment evaluates. Bitterness reacts. Discernment responds. But when you are not used to discernment, it can feel like distance, even to you.

TEACHING
Discernment is clarity without resentment.

Bitterness is rooted in unresolved anger. Discernment is rooted in wisdom. The difference is not subtle when you understand it, but it can feel subtle when you are inside the transition. Bitterness says, "I don't trust anyone." Discernment says, "I trust myself and God enough to observe before committing." Bitterness builds walls to punish others. Discernment builds boundaries to protect peace. Healing does not make you less loving. It makes you less available to what drains you. Love that is grounded in discernment does not rush intimacy. It allows consistency to speak. It values safety over chemistry.

God does not ask you to remain emotionally exposed to prove your faith. He invites you to be wise. Jesus Himself did not entrust Himself to everyone, even while loving fully. Discernment is not the absence of compassion; it is compassion guided by truth. When you feel tempted to override discernment out of fear of appearing bitter, pause. Ask yourself whether the hesitation is coming from fear or from clarity. Fear is loud and urgent. Clarity is calm and steady.

Healing matures when you stop explaining your boundaries and start trusting them. You do not owe access to prove your heart is healed. You owe yourself stewardship of the peace you worked to reclaim. Discernment is not a flaw that needs softening. It is a skill that needs honoring.

💊 Faith Prescription

Trusting Discernment Without Guilt

This week's prescription is confidence in clarity. You are prescribed permission to pause without apology and to observe without pressure. You do not need to rush to prove you are healed. You are also prescribed self-trust. Healing has refined your instincts, not damaged them.

Dosage: Pause before commitment. Observe patterns over time. No guilt-driven access.

🧬 Spiritual Vitamin

Wisdom Without Fear

Your spiritual vitamin for this chapter is wisdom. Wisdom does not rush intimacy or suppress caution.

Repeat daily: *"Discernment protects my peace."*

🕊 Holy Spirit Consult

Discerning Without Defense

Ask the Holy Spirit to help you distinguish fear-based avoidance from wisdom-based discernment. Invite Him to keep your heart soft and your boundaries strong.

🙏 Guided Prayer

"God, thank You for refining my discernment. Help me trust clarity without fearing bitterness. Teach me how to love with wisdom and protect the peace You restored. I release guilt for choosing safety. Amen."

🖉 Journal Reflection Page

1. Where do I feel tempted to override discernment to appear loving?

2. How has clarity changed the way I approach relationships?

3. What does bitterness feel like in my body versus discernment?

4. What boundaries help me stay peaceful and open?

Write until confidence replaces self-doubt.

🩺 Clinical Note

Discernment does not harden the heart. It protects it.

☑ **NEXT APPOINTMENT**

PERSONAL NOTES

Chapter 17

"Red Flags You Ignored The First Time"

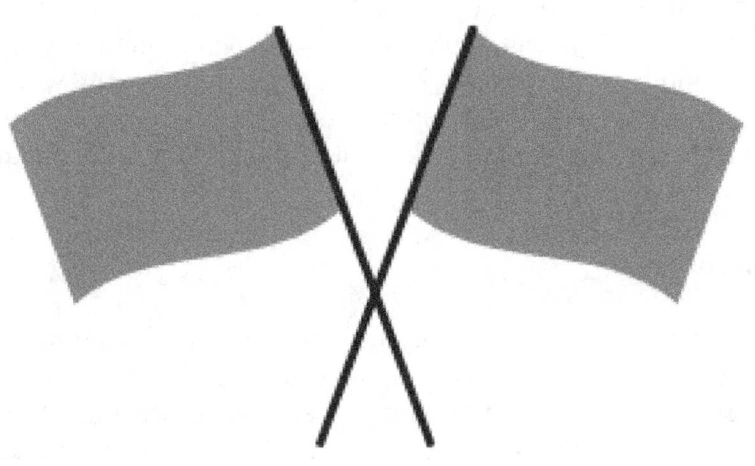

SYMPTOM
Selective memory, self-minimization, and delayed recognition of warning signs that were present early but rationalized, spiritualized, or dismissed.

One of the most humbling symptoms that surfaces in aftercare is the delayed clarity around red flags you now see clearly but did not act on the first time. This realization often arrives quietly, not as accusation, but as awareness. You look back and notice moments that made you uncomfortable, comments that felt off, behaviors that required explanation, and inconsistencies you worked hard to normalize. What once felt confusing now feels obvious.

This symptom is uncomfortable because it challenges the story you told yourself to survive the relationship. You may feel embarrassed that you ignored your intuition. You may judge yourself for staying when your body and spirit were signaling caution. You may wonder how you missed what now seems so clear. But this symptom is not about blame.

It is about learning.

Red flags are rarely dramatic. They do not show up waving signs that say "danger." They show up as subtle discomfort, small compromises, and moments you talk yourself out of trusting. You rationalize behavior because you want the connection to work. You spiritualize inconsistency because you believe in grace. You minimize your own reactions because you do not want to seem difficult or demanding.

Over time, ignoring red flags becomes a pattern of self-silencing. You override your instincts in favor of harmony. You prioritize potential over reality. You assume discomfort is something you need to work through rather than information meant to guide you. This symptom can trigger shame if misunderstood. You may ask yourself why you did not leave sooner or why you needed so much evidence to believe what you already felt. But shame is not the purpose of reflection. Growth is.

You ignored red flags because you were hopeful, not foolish. You stayed because you wanted connection, not chaos. And now, you are seeing clearly because healing has restored your discernment.

TEACHING
Red flags are not warnings of danger alone, they are invitations to self-trust.

Red flags exist to prompt curiosity, not condemnation. They are signals meant to slow you down, not shame you into retreat. The problem is not noticing red flags; the problem is explaining them away.

Healing teaches you how to sit with discomfort long enough to listen. It teaches you that intuition does not shout, it nudges. When you honor those nudges early, you protect yourself from deeper wounds later. God does not expect perfection in discernment. He expects responsiveness. When you ignore red flags repeatedly, it is often because something inside you fears loss more than misalignment. Healing addresses that fear so discernment can function freely.

Red flags are not accusations against others. They are indicators of compatibility, or the lack of it. They do not require confrontation; they require decision. You do not need proof to honor your discomfort. You need permission.

After healing, red flags become clearer because you are no longer emotionally invested in convincing yourself to stay. Your clarity is not cruelty. It is wisdom. You are not meant to analyze red flags endlessly. You are meant to respond to them appropriately. Seeing them now does not mean you failed then. It means you are wiser now.

🔖 FAITH CLINIC CLOSING
🔖 Faith Prescription

Honoring Early Discomfort

This week's prescription is early response. You are prescribed permission to slow down when something feels off without forcing explanation or resolution. Trust the pause. You are also prescribed self-compassion. Reflection is for learning, not self-punishment.

Dosage: Notice discomfort early. Pause without justification. Choose alignment over reassurance.

🧬 Spiritual Vitamin

Self-Trust

Your spiritual vitamin for this chapter is self-trust. Discernment strengthens when honored consistently.

Repeat daily: *"I trust my clarity without needing permission."*

🕊 Holy Spirit Consult

Restoring Confidence in Discernment

Ask the Holy Spirit to reinforce your trust in His guidance through your intuition and peace. Invite Him to help you respond early instead of enduring long.

🙏 Guided Prayer

"God, thank You for restoring my clarity. I release shame for what I did not know before and receive wisdom for what I see now. Teach me to honor red flags without fear and to trust Your guidance through peace. Amen."

📝 Journal Reflection Page

1. What red flags do I see clearly now?

2. How did I explain them away in the past?

3. What fear influenced my silence?

4.   How will I respond differently next time?

____

____

____

____

Writing until learning replaces regret.

⚕ Clinical Note

Red flags are not there to accuse you. They are there to protect you.

☑ **NEXT APPOINTMENT**

PERSONAL NOTES

____

____

____

____

____

____

____

____

____

____

⚕ FINAL DISCHARGE SUMMARY
Your Peace Is Not Missing, It Was Misplaced

This is not the kind of ending that comes with fireworks, applause, or a dramatic turning point. It is quieter than that. It is steadier. It is the kind of ending that does not need witnesses to be real. This is not a moment of emotional triumph; it is a moment of internal authority being restored. What you are stepping into now is not excitement. It is ownership. You did not lose your peace.

Peace is not fragile. It does not wander off when you make imperfect 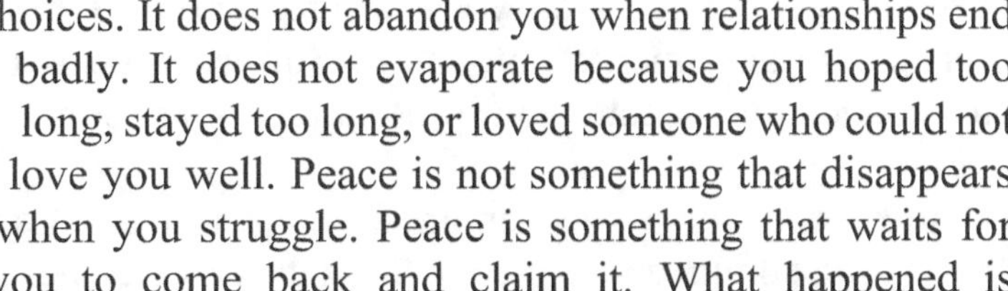 choices. It does not abandon you when relationships end badly. It does not evaporate because you hoped too long, stayed too long, or loved someone who could not love you well. Peace is not something that disappears when you struggle. Peace is something that waits for you to come back and claim it. What happened is simpler than the story you have been telling yourself, and harder than the one you were hoping for. You did not lose your peace. You **loaned** it. Slowly. Gradually. Often without realizing it. You handed it over to a connection that was never meant to carry the weight of your emotional stability, your sense of safety, or your inner calm. You let peace become conditional. You allowed it to be accessed through someone else's presence, attention, reassurance, or approval. That does not make you irresponsible. It makes you human.

You did not loan your peace because you were weak or foolish. You loaned it because you were open. You loaned it because you were hopeful. You loaned it because you were navigating a season where connection felt necessary for survival, not just companionship. You were doing the best you could with the tools you had at the time. And when peace began to feel scarce after the connection ended, you assumed something had been taken from you. Nothing was taken. Something was misplaced.

 This clinic was never about blaming you for that. It was about helping you recognize where your peace went, why it went there, and how to bring it back home without shame. The purpose of this process was not to make you colder, harder, or more guarded. It was to make you more grounded, more self-led, and more anchored than you have ever been. From the very beginning, this journey was not about erasing memory. It was about restoring authority. You were not meant to forget the relationship, the attachment, or the season you survived. You were meant to stop organizing your inner life around it. You were meant to stop letting past connections dictate your present emotional climate.

Healing, at its core, is not about amnesia. It is about reassignment. It is about taking peace out of the hands of people, patterns, and dynamics that were never meant to steward it, and returning it to the only place it can remain stable: within you. You came into this clinic carrying the quiet fear that something essential was missing. You felt unsettled, restless, and unsure of yourself. You questioned your discernment. You doubted your strength. You wondered why peace felt so far away even after you did the right thing. What you discovered along the way is that peace was never far. It was simply misplaced, waiting for you to stop reaching for it through attachment and start reclaiming it through alignment.

Throughout this process, you learned things that required courage to face. You learned that missing someone does not mean you belong to them. You learned that longing is not instruction, and that feelings can be real without being authoritative. You learned that closure is not something another person grants you through conversation, apology, or understanding. Closure is something you choose when you stop negotiating with the past.

You learned that intensity is not destiny, and that emotional fire is not the same thing as covenant. You learned that trauma bonds can feel spiritual when pain is mistaken for purpose, and that shared wounds can masquerade as sacred connection. You learned that staying too long always costs something, even when it looks like patience or faithfulness. You learned that God does not bless what He did not assign, not because He withholds goodness, but because He protects you from building your future on something temporary.

You learned that healing cannot coexist with reinforcement, and that you cannot starve an attachment while still feeding it through memory, fantasy, or access. You endured the detox season without refilling the void prematurely. You learned how to sit quietly without panicking, how to let space exist without rushing to occupy it. You discovered that forgiveness does not require reattachment, and that boundaries are not evidence of bitterness but of wisdom.

You relearned joy without emotional crutches. You discovered that joy rooted in wholeness is quieter than joy rooted in chaos, but far more durable. You learned that familiarity feels safe not because it is holy, but because it is known. You learned to trust discernment without apologizing for it. You learned to see red flags without shaming yourself for missing them before. None of that is small work. None of that is accidental. That is transformation.

There is a truth you need to hear clearly now, without softening it or over-spiritualizing it: choosing peace does not make you selfish. Choosing distance does not make you cold. Choosing yourself does not mean you chose against God. Sometimes obedience looks like staying and doing the hard work of endurance. And sometimes obedience looks like walking away, resting, and refusing to keep bleeding for something God never asked you to carry.

God is not offended by your boundaries. He helped build them. God is not disappointed by your detachment. He guided it. God is not waiting for you to return to what He helped you survive. He is inviting you forward with clarity, not backward with guilt. You are not being punished because peace feels quieter now. You are being protected because it has become steadier. Chaos always announces itself loudly. Peace does not need to prove anything. It settles. It stabilizes. It stays.

This is where many people sabotage themselves, not because they want pain back, but because quiet feels unfamiliar. Resist that urges. Quiet is not emptiness. Quiet is ownership. Now, as you prepare to leave this clinic, you are not leaving healed in the sense of being untouched by memory or immune to feeling. You are leaving healed in the sense of being *self-led*. Your emotions no longer get to assign meaning without wisdom. Your attachment no longer gets to override discernment. Your peace no longer gets to live in someone else's hands.

You are allowed to say no without explanation. You are allowed to choose distance without guilt. You are allowed to enjoy peace without justifying it. You are allowed to protect what it took you so long to rebuild.

Let this truth settle deeply: you do not owe access to proving you are healed. You do not owe availability to prove you are loving. You do not owe your peace to anyone who cannot steward it responsibly. As you move forward, old feelings may knock. Familiar patterns may try to reintroduce themselves. Guilt may whisper that you are being dramatic or selfish for maintaining boundaries. When that happens, remember this: peace is not negotiable. Peace is not a favor you grant others. It is a responsibility you carry for yourself.

You did not lose your peace. You loaned it to the wrong connection. And now, without drama, without shame, without apology, you are taking it back. Not aggressively. Not defensively. But deliberately. You are not missing anything. You are no longer chasing what never belonged to you to begin with. You are whole enough now to recognize that peace was always yours. It simply needed to be reclaimed.

You are officially discharged. And this time, you are not walking away confused or depleted. You are walking away grounded, clear, and anchored in yourself. Peace is no longer something you search for. It is something you carry. That is not an ending. That is authority restored.

PERSONAL NOTES

Epilogue

Peace Is The Life You Are Allowed To Keep

This book was never written to teach you how to leave someone. It was written to teach you how to remain with yourself without abandoning your own well-being. It was never meant to villainize a person, a relationship, or even a season that once mattered to you. Instead, it was designed to rescue your peace from being treated like collateral damage in connections that were never meant to carry the weight of your emotional stability or sense of identity.

If there is one truth that deserves to be carried with you beyond these pages, it is this: you were not broken because you stayed, and you were not weak because you hoped. You were courageous enough to leave when clarity finally outweighed attachment. Leaving did not expose your failure; it revealed your growth. It revealed that you were willing to choose wholeness over familiarity and alignment over intensity.

There was a version of you who entered that relationship believing that love required limitless sacrifice. That version of you believed endurance was a spiritual virtue and that confusion was simply part of destiny unfolding. That version of you mistook emotional intensity for intimacy and attachment for purpose. None of that makes you foolish. It means you were learning in real time what wisdom often teaches only after loss and experience. You were doing the best you could with the understanding you had at the time.

Now, however, you stand as someone different. You are no longer dependent on chaos to feel alive or on validation to feel secure. You no longer need to borrow peace from another person to feel grounded. You have learned something essential that reshapes how you approach every relationship and decision going forward: peace is not a reward you earn after surviving pain, but a standard you use to choose what belongs in your life next.

The healing you have done was not meant to harden you or make you distant. It was meant to make you honest. Honest about what drains you internally, even if it looks acceptable externally. Honest about what destabilizes you emotionally, even if it appears harmless on the surface. Honest about the cost of certain connections, even when those connections once felt meaningful. You are not less loving now; you are simply more discerning about where your love is placed. That discernment is not selfishness. It is stewardship.

Peace is not passive, fragile, or weak. Peace is active and discerning. It requires alignment to survive. It refuses to coexist with ongoing confusion or emotional compromise. Peace does not stay in environments where it must justify itself, and it does not remain in relationships where it is treated as optional. When peace leaves, it does not punish you. It protects you. It leaves first because it recognizes misalignment before your mind is ready to name it.

The moment your peace began to slip away was not the moment you failed. It was the moment your soul recognized a truth your heart had not yet accepted. That persistent discomfort you tried to pray away was not spiritual weakness; it was  wisdom attempting to get your attention. That restlessness you could not silence was not rebellion; it was discernment asking for space to speak.

Now you know how to listen. You are no longer impressed by chemistry that lacks consistency, nor persuaded by words that produce no lasting fruit. You no longer feel obligated to label suffering as growth simply to avoid the grief of letting go. You have learned that not everything intense is meaningful and not everything familiar is safe. You have learned that love does not require self-erasure, and faith does not demand emotional harm. You have learned that God is not glorified by your exhaustion and that obedience does not require you to disappear. Perhaps most importantly, you have learned that peace is a responsibility. It is something you protect intentionally, honor consistently, and no longer loan out casually. Peace is not something you stumble into; it is something you steward with wisdom and care. As you move forward, there may still be moments when old patterns feel tempting or when loneliness speaks in convincing tones. Familiarity may knock softly, asking for just a little access or one more explanation. When that happens, remember the work it took to get here. Remember the clarity you fought to regain. Remember that healing is not measured by how much you can tolerate, but by how clearly you can choose alignment when it matters most.

You are allowed to walk away from anything that costs you your peace. You are allowed to rest without defending your decision. You are allowed to build a life that feels quiet and grounded, even if it seems unremarkable to people who thrive in chaos. That is not settling. That is stability, and stability is sacred.

You are not required to relieve old pain to prove that you learned from it. You are not obligated to reopen doors to demonstrate forgiveness. You are not required to remain accessible in order to be loved. Your growth does not need witnesses, and your boundaries do not need applause. Your peace does not need permission.

This is the life you are allowed to keep: a life where peace is not dependent on who is present, a life where joy is steady rather than explosive, a life where discernment is trusted instead of questioned, and a life where survival is no longer mistaken for purpose. You did not lose your peace. You did not fail love. You did not misunderstand God. You simply outgrew what could not accompany you into the next season of your life.

Now you move forward with clarity instead of chaos, with wholeness instead of attachment, and with peace that finally rests where it always belonged. You move forward without rushing, without chasing, and without explaining yourself. You move forward grounded, whole, and free enough to choose differently when it matters. This is not the end of your story. It is the beginning of a life led by peace.

PERSONAL NOTES

ABOUT THE AUTHOR

Dr. Patricia Tanner was born and raised in Sanford FL. She comes from a family of three siblings. Patricia Tanner is the founder of Multhai International Realty, Multhai Asset Management Services, and Multhai Investment Group which is located in Sanford, Florida. She is a graduate of the University of Central Florida, where she received a Bachelor of Science in Business Administration and a minor in Human Resources Management.

Dr. Tanner began her career shortly thereafter as a Regional Property Manager in the apartment community. Throughout her career in property management, she has built interpersonal relationships with corporate clients. She has a successful track record of increasing company revenues over $5 million annually, through hard work, commitment, creativeness, and strategic planning.

Her experience and leadership role eventually led her to achieve a Florida Real Estate Broker license. She spent fifteen years in the Real Estate field while completing a Master of Arts in Human Resources Management from Webster University, and a Master of Public Administration from Troy University. It was in this capacity that she decided to open her own brokerage company, Multhai International Realty.

In addition, Dr. Tanner finds time in her busy schedule to participate in her own Non-For-Profit Organization, Stones 2 Homes. She remains President of her organization in which she helps people build, keep, or purchase homes in affordable communities. She is the founder of PNT Property Partners in which she buys vacant land, develops it, and constructs brand new construction homes in Sanford Florida. Her overall goal is to educate and provide resources to help people overcome financial hardships and credit disadvantage to live the American Dream through homeownership in spite of economic hardship. Through her visions she will continue to grow as an entrepreneur and is willing to share her knowledge, experience, and expertise with anyone who is willing to learn.

MORE BOOKS BY THE AUTHOR

Welcome to the Faith Clinic—where your soul doesn't need to be perfect to be healed.

You've smiled through burnout. Quoted scripture while quietly unraveling. Prayed, fasted, and still felt like your faith flatlined. If that's you, Faith Clinic: Volume I is your spiritual prescription.

Dr. Patricia S. Tanner—known as The Faith Doctor—invites you into a raw, grace-filled recovery journey for the soul. With 7 powerful doses of faith-infused wisdom, this book delivers healing where performance failed and offers truth where church hurt left a scar. Designed especially for spiritually exhausted youth and young adults, each "dose" reads like an IV drip of hope for believers secretly running on empty.

You don't need to be okay to show up. You just need to be willing. The clinic is open.

NOW AVAILABLE:

www.amazon.com

Healing was just the beginning. Now it's time to grow.

If Faith Clinic Volume I met you in crisis, Volume II meets you in recovery. Because faith isn't a one-time fix—it's a lifestyle that needs maintenance, accountability, and consistency. Welcome to your follow-up care plan.

In Faith Clinic: Volume II, Dr. Patricia S. Tanner—aka The Faith Doctor—guides you through the next level of your spiritual healing journey. From navigating church trauma and burnout to facing silence from God and rediscovering purpose, this book goes deeper than devotionals. It's not about hype—it's about habits that sustain real, lasting transformation.

With raw wisdom, relatable stories, and no-shame truths, each chapter is a spiritual check-in for believers who want to thrive—not just survive. Whether you're wrestling with doubt, craving stability, or simply ready to grow up in God, this clinic is for you.

You've detoxed. Now it's time to build. Let's get you discharge-ready.

NOW AVAILABLE:
www.amazon.com

Welcome to the Faith Clinic: Anxiety Edition, where God doesn't coddle your coping mechanisms but confronts them with surgical precision.

This book is for the ones who love Jesus but still can't sleep. For the worship leaders crying in church bathrooms. For the believers who pray in spirals, fight shame on Sundays, and secretly think, "Maybe I'm the only one who can't seem to breathe through this." You're not crazy. You're just in a fight — and this book is your spiritual triage.

Inside you'll find:

- Panic attacks in pews and the prayers that still work.
- Scriptures that talk you off the ledge.
- What to do when you feel numb and God feels quiet.
- How to walk out of shame loops, judgment spirals, and performance religion.

This isn't just encouragement. It's equipment.
Because healing isn't a moment — it's a walk.

NOW AVAILABLE:
www.amazon.com

Welcome to the Faith Clinic: Stress Edition — where we don't hand you cute verses and clichés. We hand you spiritual prescriptions for real pressure, real panic, and real prayers from tired believers holding it together by a thread.

This book is for the overwhelmed—those trusting God while juggling bills, burnout, hustle culture, and holy frustration. If you've ever whispered, "God, are You even watching this mess?" this is for you.

Inside you'll find raw, soul-hitting chapters like:

- "God, I Trust You, But These Bills Keep Coming"
- "If Rest Is Holy, Why Does It Feel Like Slacking?"
- "I'm Tired of Smiling So You Won't Worry"

This isn't fluff. It's real talk for real stress—and a reminder that you're not forgotten, you're being fortified.

The Faith Clinic is open. Breathe in & take your spiritual vitamins. Healing begins here.

NOW AVAILABLE:
www.amazon.com

This isn't just a feeling; it's a flare signal from the soul. You pray, serve, and believe in God, but something deep inside is still simmering. Welcome to the Faith Clinic: Anger Edition, where suppressed emotions meet sacred intervention.

In this volume, Dr. Patricia S. Tanner guides you through spiritual triage for:

- Silent rage and emotional suppression
- The grief–anger connection
- Rejection wounds from childhood to church hurt

This isn't a lecture. It's a spiritual detox. No shame. No sugar-coating. Just raw, honest healing. Whether you're snapping at loved ones or silently seething under the surface, this book meets you at the boiling point—and leads you to the breakthrough.

This is the clinic.

This is your moment.

And God is ready to heal the anger behind your amen.

NOW AVAILABLE:

www.amazon.com

In this powerful installment of the Faith Clinic series, Dr. Patricia S. Tanner brings biblical insight, emotional compassion, and spiritual strength to those walking through grief. Designed as a healing chamber for the soul, each "dose" of this devotional targets a different dimension of sorrow, guiding you from pain to peace, from mourning to joy.

Inside, you'll discover:

- Daily doses of Scripture-based encouragement.
- Personal reflections and prayers for each stage of grief.
- Practical faith prescriptions to help you process loss and find purpose.

Whether you are navigating the recent loss of a loved one, confronting buried grief from the past, or supporting someone else in their sorrow, this devotional offers a gentle yet powerful roadmap to healing. Come, take your seat in the Faith Clinic—where the Great Physician is ready to restore your soul.

NOW AVAILABLE:

www.amazon.com

30 Days Of Grieving

Given By The Inspiration Of God

Healing From COVID-19

Almost a year later, it hit me... My mother was gone, and I was still stuck at the hospital. I had tried everything from crying to counseling, and even prayer. Pray they told me. Trust God they insisted. But it seemed as if nothing was working. I was hurt, dealing with my reality: my mother was not coming back.

While journeying through grief, it was under the divine 'Inspiration of God' that He placed me in a trance. While I was gaining a revelation about grief, He gave me this journal, '30 Days Of Grieving.'

NOW AVAILABLE:
www.amazon.com

The 30 Days Challenge:

I Tested POSITIVE for COVID-19

If you had 30 days to live, what would you do? If you were told that you needed to prepare for a marathon in 30 days and you were completely out of shape, what would you do first? If a family member handed you one million dollars and told you that you had to figure out how to build a house (debt free), how would you execute your plan?

I'm catching you off guard with these requests, right? Well, this is exactly what COVID-19 did when it snatched my mother's life away, wrecking my entire world. I had to battle for my mother AND my faith in 30 days flat. What a challenge!

Throughout this book, I will walk you through my brief journey with COVID-19, negative of a happy ending. I will share the diary I kept while attending to my mother, and the scriptures I read, prayed, and quoted as my shield and protection.

Take the journey with me, there is healing on the other side!

NOW AVAILABLE:

www.amazon.com

Can Salvation Get You Into Heaven? The Answer Is Yes! offers a powerful and biblically grounded exploration of God's eternal plan, revealing the heart of the Gospel and the assurance of salvation through Jesus Christ.

Unpacking life's most vital questions—Who is God? Why were we created? What does Jesus' life mean for us?—this book brings clarity to the believer's journey and confirms that salvation, once received, is eternally secure.

Whether you're seeking understanding or affirming your faith, this inspiring guide will lead you into the confidence and joy of knowing heaven is your eternal home.

NOW AVAILABLE:

www.amazon.com

What happens when the Kingdom becomes a stranger?

The Godless Climb is not a rejection of faith—it is a raw, unflinching journey through what remains when belief unravels. With brutal honesty and tender grace, this book explores the spiritual free fall that follows the loss of divine certainty, the ache of unanswered prayers, and the void left when God no longer feels near.

Written for those who have quietly slipped out of the pews and into a wilderness of doubt, grief, and inner searching, this is not a triumph story—but a survival story. A confession. A sacred wrestle. Through personal reflection and prophetic insight, the author unpacks what it means to climb without a safety net, to live without the scaffolding of religious performance, and to build a new compass in the absence of old crutches.

You haven't arrived. But you're still climbing. And that is holy.

NOW AVAILABLE:
www.amazon.com

It Was The God In

Me

Success can be attributed to many things. Depending on the person who has obtained success would determine those to whom they attribute their success. Some give credit to their daily routine while others give credit to a mentor or some sort of system they followed. When I think about my success, the only person who I can give the credit to is God.

In this memoir, I share the successes and failures I have experienced throughout my life. From my individual experiences to my entrepreneurial journey, I share how God has walked with me every step of the way.

Come and see.. It Was The God In Me!!

NOW AVAILABLE:
www.amazon.com

The Triple 7 Formula is designed for business owners who are looking forward to hitting the million-dollar mark in their business. If you own a business and seem to be running in financial circles, this book will get you on track to simultaneously gaining sound business structure and millions in your bank account.

It was through many conversations with business owners lacking financial gain that prompted Patricia to share her blueprint for millionaire status. Through this book, she demonstrates how to gain financial ground by developing strong teams, implementing systems, and setting stackable goals. If you are ready to gain a laser sharp focus, and implement these clear steps, you will position yourself for financial greatness. Your business will be sound, and you will see financial growth beyond your wildest dreams!!

NOW AVAILABLE:
www.amazon.com

The Triple 7 Formula is specifically crafted for business owners aspiring to reach the million-dollar milestone. If you are a business owner feeling stuck in financial cycles, this book will set you on the path to building both a solid business structure and financial success.

This workbook is designed to complement the textbook of the same name. As you progress through its pages, you will be inspired to take decisive steps toward becoming a millionaire. From constructing your business framework to creating the millionaire's avatar, this process will expand your knowledge and mindset. Not only will you chart a course to financial success, but you will also identify your accountability circle and select a mentor to guide you toward greatness.

I cannot guarantee millionaire status unless you actively follow the steps to begin your journey. If you are searching for a get rich quick scheme, this workbook is not for you. I am looking for those ready to put in the effort—and since you are reading this, I believe that's you!

You have finally found it: Your roadmap to millions!

NOW AVAILABLE:
WWW.Amazon.com

Find Patricia on The Web:

www.PatriciaTanner.com

Follow Patricia on social media:

Facebook & Instagram: @PatriciaTannerInc